More Advance Praise for *Siteseeing*

"In this heart-to-heart conversation, poets Ariel Gordon and Brenda Schmidt document the broken beauty of a world in crisis. Rooted in place and powered by precise observation, these generous poems will speak to you wherever you do your own siteseeing." — Candace Savage, author of *A Geography of Blood: Unearthing history in a prairie landscape.*

"If you've ever listened in to someone else's conversation or read a letter not addressed to you, this compelling collection is for you. Written with the fresh wit of texts and the wisdom of window-staring, their perspicacious observations spread roots under our restless feet and their truths are bright leaves sheltering us from the scorch of drought and the drench of rain. When future generations ask what it was like to live through the 2020s, this poetic correspondence cawed, roared and hooted from either side of an impassable prairie must absolutely be pressed into their hands." — Joanna Lilley, author of *Endlings*

Siteseeing

To Sheila—
I loved your poem!
Thanks so much for
Sharing...
Poetry forever!

Siteseeing

Writing nature & climate across the prairies

Ariel Gordon
Brenda Schmidt

AT BAY
press

WINNIPEG

Siteseeing

Copyright © 2023 Ariel Gordon and Brenda Schmidt

Design and layout by Matt Stevens and M. C. Joudrey
Cover art by M. C. Joudrey
Eastern Tailed Blue butterfly photograph by M. C. Joudrey

Published by At Bay Press October 2023.

Library and Archives Canada cataloguing in publication is available upon request.

ISBN 978-1-998779-04-8

Printed and bound in Canada.

This book is printed on acid free paper that is 100% recycled ancient forest friendly (100% post-consumer recycled).

First Edition

10 9 8 7 6 5 4 3 2 1

atbaypress.com

How to Sitesee: an Introduction
by Ariel Gordon & *Brenda Schmidt*

In early 2021, I worked the back end of a Zoom event for J.R. Léveillé and E.D. Blodgett's French-English poetry collaboration, *Ex Nihilo*. I came away from the event like a neon sign that had been turned on, alternately buzzing and humming. So I contacted the person who helped me install that sign in the first place, Brenda Schmidt.

I met Brenda back in 2003 at Fred Wah's poetry colloquium at Sage Hill. At the time, she had one book to her name and I was seven years away from my debut. In the years that followed, though she called herself my friend, she acted like a mentor, introducing me around, suggesting I do/*not* do things, supporting me however she could. We were a province apart but she was a wonderful light to have on my literary horizon.

So it was midnight, almost twenty years after our first meeting, when I emailed Brenda, asking if she maybe wanted to try something similar to *Ex Nihilo*?

Now the author of five books of poetry and a book of essays, Brenda is also laser-focused on birds, gardening, and photography. I am a bit tree-obsessed but also love mushrooming and mudlarking.

I proposed that she write on birds and the environment, while I would focus on trees and the environment. I proposed that we'd alternate.

For some reason, she said yes.

Specifically, she said: "Exciting! Short is good. Form unnecessary. Just gimme some rules or whatnot and I'll follow your lead."

I started with a short-ish poem, she responded with same, and that was it. That was our nod to the renga form, as viewed through Blodgett's and Leveille's window. Sometimes, we wrote two poems a day. Sometimes a week went by without a poem, one or both of us busy.

We wrote together for a year, moving from a polar vortex through a drought reeking of wildfire to a big snow year. Our poems got longer; either we grew tired of the constraint or we just relaxed into the exchange.

It was a hard, pandemic-ed, climate-changed year but, reading through these poems, I think we captured so much of the broken loveliness that is available to us as residents of the Canadian prairies.

I named the project *Siteseeing* because the point was to focus on what was available to us: on our immediate surroundings, on the local. Sightseeing is usually something you do when you're travelling. But with travel no longer an option, I wondered if siteseeing was something that could be done while sheltering in place.

Spending focused time with writers is always generative.

I knew from the moment I met her that Ariel is a leader, a community builder who digs right in and makes things happen.

I am more solitary and more inclined to sit back.

At Sage Hill in 2003, Ariel won the coveted can of potatoes in recognition of her leadership skills that led to the successful completion of a chapbook of poems written and built by the group. I struggled to sew the pages. I mostly kept to myself.

Reading through these poems, I can't help but think of the coyote and badger video that went viral a couple years back. It's night. A coyote standing in the mouth of a culvert is doing that playful bounce and tail wag move meaning follow me! Into the frame comes a badger moving cautiously at first. Coyotes and badgers are known to hunt together, but this was the first time I've seen them interact. Like the badger who trusted the coyote, I followed Ariel into the uncertainty of these times, knowing there would be light, knowing the pleasure of digging deep into place together would sustain us both. Tail up, I waddled after her as fast as I could go.

I'd follow her anywhere.

The thing about writing *Siteseeing* for me was the dailyness of it. After one of Brenda's poems arrived, I would take stock: what had I seen that day, on my walks or from my window? Knowing I had a poem to write today and tomorrow and next week got me outside more often that I might have otherwise. When it was +/- 35 degrees out, and I was stuck inside, sad and frustrated, sick of my house and my neighbourhood, the humidity hanging like a chandelier above me, I would report on what I hadn't seen. Or what was visible through the screens of my social media feeds.

I have always found social media to be a site of connection. It's how I've kept in touch with my writing friends from across the country. I work hard to connect with people, to be vulnerable, but I also use social media to share my enthusiasm for the world. If there was a transcript of my social media, it would read something like: "Loooooooook at this photo of a tree/mushroom/broken bottle/shadow/nest/nut."

I want to help people notice the world, to see and appreciate it while there's still time. It strikes me that this is more important than ever, given our climate crisis.
I also do it because I have aphantasia. Which is to say,

the only thing I see when I close my eyes is the back of my eyelids and/or darkness. So I rely on photographs to remember details and take a lot of photos when out in nature. But that doesn't distance me from nature. It helps me feel more connected to the natural world.

What helped me to feel connected while writing *Siteseeing* was remembering to acknowledge receipt. Otherwise, one of us would be convinced, CONVINCED, that the poem in question had gone missing or had been declared spam.

My normal process is to write first/second/tenth drafts of poems over months, based in equal parts on moments of inspiration and exercises I set for myself. My *Siteseeing* poems were written shockingly quickly, sometimes when I was binging TV or in bed, but the difference was, I was writing them for an audience I admired very much. I had to live up to Brenda's badger standard.

Like for many, the pandemic has had a numbing effect on me. Time is weirder than ever before. I could float along for days, weeks, and months and write not a word.

Siteseeing *grounded me again. The incredible details in Ariel's poems brushed the dust off my senses and soon I was looking more closely at the passing of each day. Her playfulness made me laugh, her line breaks gave me energy. When I sat down to write back, the leaps came naturally. I wrote almost every poem on my phone and then logged in to webmail to check it against hers. The connections were always there.*

The back and forth awakened my competitive side as well. I wanted Ariel with her keen coyote senses to experience the moose and deer, porcupines and grasshoppers. I wanted her to sit with me as I moaned about the heat and stressed about the lack of water. I wanted to hear her groan at my terrible puns.

I didn't want my poems to pale next to the vibrancy of hers. I knew she'd sniff out any sidestepping.

I also have almost no sense of smell.

But I try to trust in the process of writing poems...and soon realized that writing *these* poems allowed me to empty myself out, to unburden myself. I knew it was good for my mental health to pay attention, every day, to what was around me.

But I will say that when our back-and-forth ended, 203 poems later, I could still feel the itch of a *Siteseeing* poem building like a headache behind my eyes.

I know I will miss writing to Brenda, poet to poet, mentor to manatee, Saskatchewan-ite (Saskatchewan-arian?) to Manitoban, birder to treehugger. She was my roommate in every stanza we wrote, this lonely/intimate year, and I am looking forward to inhabiting other rooms with her, airing this work…

Which is to say: *HONK!*

Coyotes and badgers don't always hunt together.

I know of two active badger hole complexes nearby. One is a short walk east of here on the other side of the slough. The other is across the road in the barnyard, just south of where the pig barns once stood. A badger has lived on that hillside for as long as I can remember. A few weeks after the fire, I noticed freshly dug dirt in a place of soot. The badger had survived.

It's mid-March already. I have yet to hear geese. I could write a poem about that, or I could simply stare out the window. I can see the hillside from here. I imagine the badger will sit alone on the hump of dirt at the mouth of its hole, watching the odd coyote trot along the facing hillside, always up to something.

Behind that coyote is another coyote.

Standing at the axis of hydro pole
& hundred-year-old elm,
head back, I resolve

three dark lumps
against a February sky,
a wickerwork of winter

branches & wires into owls,
then wind-whipped plastic bags,
then bickering

squirrels. Bark rains down.
Tell me, who shape-shifted?
Me? Them?

Fifty feet up in the cottonwood
two ravens wing to wing
on a branch reaching over the drifts

twist bills into breasts
leisurely, throat feathers blooming
under the three pm sun.

They pause. One eyes the adjacent
branch broken during the blizzard
of blizzards. The other wipes its bill

on snow at its feet & eyes me.
Between us the still-slim buds
point up, grasping almost.

During the polar vortex,
a friend's linden cracked
like the spine of a favourite book

in the deep cold. I windowed
my boulevard elm while the "persistent,
large-scale cyclone" spun,

an uneven chunk of wood
on a lathe, the continent shaking.
As the Arctic Ocean warms, tell me:

How do you over-winter?

How do you widow a tree?

Water drips, the snow finally sinking.
A thin string of deer ignores me
as they head past ragged maples,

less than half the herd it was. They go
to sleep beneath the neighbour's
front room window. Safe, at least,

one of the triplets, ice hanging from its jaw
never woke up, I'm told. Its siblings
trot by now, necks pulled back,

mouths hanging open. There's nothing
I can do. Twigs rise & fall
in the switching wind.

The snow/ice loud under my boots—
dense like styrofoam, durable
like metal, under

the swish of my snowpants.
My mask's loops fastened to my hair
with ice. This weekend?

The forecast calls for +9 C
but I don't know how to walk

when the world trips

like a breaker between freeze
& thaw. Yes, I'm afraid of falls but
most of all: new buds/bugs freezing.

Seventeen geese fly by my window.
Do they see me
making my bed?

March 4th. I count again to be sure
as they set down on a hill
almost free of snow

to eat red lentils
the combine didn't get last fall.
It was a good crop, the field

sprayed four times: herbicide,
fungicide, fungicide, desiccant.
Up goes the comforter.

I walked a sunny ditch full of mulch
& sawdust after forty Manitoba maples
& willows, mature

trees that had set themselves up
under power lines

at the edge of a park

were mowed down. They say blackouts
& power interruptions. They say volunteer
& scrub. What they mean?

Bucket trucks & chippers now
& herbicides later. It smelled glorious,
it felt awful.

The maples in the yard, snapped
twenty feet up, die
with dignity

each a gothic castle,
a church, spires pointing
out my lack of control

over the future. Some I grew
up with, some were just keys
when I left not knowing

one day I'd be back. House
sparrows stuff belfries with ditch grass
& chirp emphatically

whether I'm here or not.
I can't take down
trees so holey.

Twice, the Widowmaker has dropped
hefty limbs onto the boulevard
& what's left hangs out

over the road like a dare.
Woodpeckers love it—sundialing holes
around the cut edge—

but I take care not to park
under it when the wind rises.
My Wolseley elm leans

over the house a little more
every year, its seedlings competing
with volunteer Manitoba maple

& Creeping Charlie
in the unmade beds below.

A moose climbs a drift
more than a moose high
not once breaking through

crowns
of willow & dogwood
now in reach.

The slough will be
full this spring

unlike last spring

& the moose
I watch from inside
will hole up & eat.

Early spring & snow-eating
temps have me perched
on my porch

when an entire flock
of sparrows enters the beat-up
cedar & spindly lilac

in front of the house: *Cheep!*
Cheep! I am always falling up
weather's stairs,

asking warm spells
& cold snaps: Are you climate
changed? *Cheep!*

Yesterday herds of deer
grazed the hilltops
now mostly bare of snow

upwards of eighty
heads up, heads down,

some marching

over drifts
right up to the house.
Yes I'm still here.

Today just one
lies in view, magpies
cleaning off its ribs.

Naked limbs white
against the new blue
of a warm spring afternoon—

dying cottonwood in a high wind.
Bits of silvery bark in the brown
grass between my feet.

On a snag, last summer's kite,
a bundle of pink plastic.
It rustles, remembering flight,

my brown eyes already blown
to the next dying cottonwood.

March ends much
the way it began
if I remember. Correct me.

If I am song I am
the song of the American
tree sparrow, a flocking

song, I think, but right now
they call out in alarm as I
build a bunny out of snow

the storm left behind two
days ago. It's hard. The ears
keep breaking off.

The great horned owls hoot
at each other from neighbouring
branches of graveyard spruce.

The ground littered with loot:
intact pellets & ones spilling small
bones & tufts of regurgitated fur.

(Underground, lateral roots
& disintegrating
boxes of big bones...) *Hoots!*

More *Hoots!* But it's April
& they haven't nested. Were they spooked
by that March heat-wave?

Are they done?

9

Are we?

April fools! The day
with or without the apostrophe
melts into all the rest.

The sun sets as the cats & I
watch a pair of geese circle
the house & land honk honk

on the hill in plain view
clearly taken with me
& my "Hello goosey goosey!"

I feel bird. Water
drips, runs. The cats stiffen.
The wind dies down.

Barred feathers tangled in the brown
down of last year's leaves.
You can't own

owl parts but ejecta doesn't count
so I find myself baking batches
of pellets. The house smells

mucky & sour but my bird-brained
partner always asks:

"Hey, what's cooking?"

The rocking chair creaks
the back & forth
for hours,

the burnt-up yard
across the road
closer & farther.

Great view
of the still-standing
chicken house

with its plywood exterior
walls painted red
back in the days of lead

& new metal roof we nailed
over curled cedar shingles
to keep the rain off the cats.

With a good arm
I could ding the metal
from here.

Hounded from perch to perch,
as people lurched across the graveyard,

holding their phones overhead

like they were searching
for Wi-Fi. Or the waning moon.
We'd stood in the brown grass

for an hour & all we got
was *Hoot*ed conversation, the owls
hidden. M's golden eye drifted

to mine, then he slow-blinked.
Meaning, "The owls don't owe us
anything, eh?" I rattled the coins

in my pocket in response.
In the road, red-eyed
traffic streamed by, reliable.

Steady wings overhead
thousands upon thousands
of wings pumping wind—

Snow geese, Ross's geese
Greater white-fronted geese
Cackling geese, Canada geese

all calling at once. Hello
I think, but don't call back,
for fear of interference or not

being heard. A lone bird flaps
off to the side like it's embarrassed.
I focus. A short-eared owl!

An ambulance siren chirps
like a bird outside my window,
keeping the flock in contact.

It's been a year of sheltering in place
with a cat up each nostril,
but I've been escaping

outside to visit trees,
holding pieces of clear-
cut trees up

to the camera
as activism. Is that sawdust
onscreen or just stray pixels? I swipe

& a rescued
red-tailed hawk swoops
from my phone

to my laptop, purely
for educational purposes.

Someone posts crocuses

on Facebook & we are out the door
& across the pasture

wind be damned, sleeping
deer too who boing boing
from slough to hilltop & turn

stunned. Are we real
or some kind of nightmare?
Both I suppose. Just look

at our rubber boots. Dry
most of the way. Finally
we find a single crocus. One.

Last year. Ejected from the house
like seeds to be dispersed,
explosive, we drove

to a park, whose blown-in
litter distracted from the hairy flowers
on hairy stems

of lilac-throated prairie crocuses.
(I nearly cried.) The far side
all flooded

trails & booters but also bare
branches festooned

with bittersweet

vines, the empty seed pods
vivid orange. I felt collected
until someone asked:

"Is that the invasive kind?"

The place seemed fine
the last I looked, the snow
in the yard sinking fast

bare patches of grass showing
a tinge of green. I spend
an hour planting sweet peas

in mud where the drift has shrunk away
& the earth sank a foot
in the trench. If I push too hard

the seeds will sprout & root
around the waterline. I was warned
the dirt will take years to settle.

Last year, I choked on crocus posts,
my shoulders up around my ears
as case counts climbed like

kudzu vines. Last spring, bedroom
communities along the Red River Valley
ring-diked as they waited for the water

to crest. This year, it's drought,
the river's gumbo shoulders bare
& shivery. Grassfires & variants of concern.

And crocuses? I find myself collecting
other people's pictures
like they were seed packets.

I strike the earth again
& again with the rake
& again until I think

my arms will break
right off & fall
in the mess of dead

borage stems. Pause
to remove fistfuls
of clay from the tines. Plant

as soon as the ground can
be worked, the packet says.
Cover lightly with dirt.

Tomorrow, I will drag out the hose
& sit on my front steps
while it gushes

wintry water from Shoal Lake 40
all over the roots of my old elm.
I will be tempted

to drink from the cold metal hose.
I will notice that the stairs need
painting, my boots

dusty. But! Downy fiddleheads
in the garden. Merlins
Shriek-ing

overhead.

21 degrees, 13 percent humidity
with wind gusts over 50,
when smoke goes up

like something blew up
just over the hill. I shake
as I call H to the window.

"I'm seeing right, right?"
A truck flies by. We grab the keys
grab the spades & run

for the truck & mount
the hill at speed. There we see
the source ten miles away.

Ten years ago, M was tuned
into the absurd radio
of the police scanner: ninjas, machetes,

parking lot brawls. He'd call
to say: "There's a report of a fire
in the next street—look out

the back door & tell me
if I should send a photographer."
Our daughter sleeping upstairs,

I'd open the door: sirens,
train squeal, cars rattling
down the midnight alley. I'd look

at the lilac we planted
too close to the house,
the sky pregnant with thunder.

"I guess there's smoke," I'd say.

The willow, older than me, is near
the end of its life.

A starling watches me clean

its leavings off the chair
I set too close to its nest hole.
If I interpret this right

the starling hopes I drop sooner.
Here's how. I believe it
& its cronies sitting up there

mimicking red-tails, killdeer
& back-up alarms
murmurate with me in mind.

On my goosey commute to campus, the grey
tube socks of trembling aspen
catkins sway back

& forth on branches, rain-washed
laundry. The soft grey light has forced
the dogwood to go

lipstick red in the shrub layer.
There is nothing
better than new growth —

charged filaments glowing yellow
on old grey willows—
I didn't know I needed.

The geese & I miss you.
HONK!

I don't know what to do
with all the deadwood.
Enough to build a barn.

It would cost thousands
to have chainsaws
come in & get it done.

It's supposed to rain. Please
rain. My gut burns, rains acid.
Enough holes to house a flock

of birds. Even starlings could fit
their egos inside some of them.
Had I any sense I'd walk.

I got word today after my walk
that the vigil for the maples & willows,
their wallets fat with shade,

was clearcut: more & more variants
of concern in our case counts—
it's not wise to gather

around seeping stumps & mourn,

be human together
in the rain-damped grass.

Bureaucracy, drought. It doesn't matter
how or why. You planted groves
of trees. You spent

hours digging deep holes.
I'm standing with you now,
keening.

A good hundred blackbirds,
a mixed flock, largely
red-winged, dot

the top of the tallest cottonwood
& sing. All face the same
west.

The wind waves all about wildly
before taking a bough. I laugh
at my little joke, go on

listening.

Another Saturday night, another nest.
This one, a trembling aspen
with two owlets

bobbing in & out of its deep pocket.
There is forty meters of brush
between us & the tree.

It's dusk, teens & dog-walkers
everywhere. I keep focusing on budding
twigs instead of her back-lit

ear tufts. I cough into
my cupped hand & her head whips
around. *Eeep!*

Whatever happened last night
hunkers down today, waiting
out the storm. The flock of blackbirds

perch low in the chokecherry,
face the wind, their bills
stabbing snowflakes. Snowflakes

don't care. There's a meme about
that somewhere. Isn't there?
The power will go out soon,

I'm sure. The phone is charging,
the heat is cranked. The blackbirds
ride the gusts to the end.

Storm coming.
Compton tortoiseshells
beat like little flames

at the windows
of rooms that were locked
all winter.

The word is out: a cluster
of variants in the area.
The community bulletin

board hops with calls for
transparency, decency, privacy.
I refresh the page. Over & over

blackbirds drop to the snow,
scoop up seed then fly up
in alarm.

After the storm, we peered over
the rail of the love-locked
train bridge

to the little mud island
below: a goose nesting in snow
as though

it was goose down
or cattail fluff. A flippered trail led
from river to snowed-in nest,

from bicycle tires to grocery
carts to dock moorings
half-buried in gumbo.

The gander must
have thought our attention
unseemly, because he swam over,

HONK-ing, but we'd already given
up, our cameras
refusing to focus

on her small black head.

I train my eyes
on the feeder like I do
each morning.

The blackbirds continue
to clean up the seed
except for the millet.

The grackles have a thing
for corn. It's gone
but they're not,

for gluttons
don't just stop
consuming, do we?

I feel full though, almost
content. The flock seems ok
with my distance.

Dog & deer & rabbit prints, movement
frozen for the moment,
the snow & ice & snirt slated

to be gone by the weekend.
The university's a ghost town,
a goose town, mating pairs

standing around like missing
students, motion-
activated sculpture.

A man in a sedate trenchcoat
climbed by a gander
like he was a ladder

next to a parking lot nest.
He stared at me, envying my wide
berth, his ribs cancelled

like a passport.

There's one less blackbird
& one full hawk, sharp-shinned
I think. I won't go into it, though I will

say my camera's shutter speed,
while high, is nothing compared
to my shudder while I watch

it unfold. Teeth chattering,
the cat slams the window, knowing
a deal when it sees one. It's BOGO

season after all. When the hawk flies
off, the red-wing hanging, I open
the window & the cat is gone.

Someone posts to the Manitoba Wildlife
group, elated, that they heard
a merlin shriek

in the next street. "RIP songbirds,"
someone replies, having invested
heavily in black oil

seed & squirrel-proof mesh. Having
invested, like all of us, in cities
& gasoline. As if

all those choices

aren't killing millions
of birds— palm warbler strikes

the lit windows of the HSBC bank,
yellow-bellied sapsucker
the APTN building—

nevermind pesticide
pyramid schemes. As if
an intact ecosystem doesn't need

all the rungs of the ladder:
grass + rabbits + foxes.
Insects + songbirds + merlins,

Shriek-ing lustily
at prey, at each other,
as they hunt the budding treetops.

Or as I posted: "Everything's
gotta eat." (And then, I liked
my own comment.)

The wood frogs calling
at the tip of the drift grow
quiet as the semi comes

over the hill, wings of dust
spreading over the fields.

The blackbirds fly for cover,

I run for the door, the chair
rocking as the semi roars
by without slowing down.

How will it make the corner
ahead? The glyphosate it hauls
will slosh something awful.

Yesterday's heart-attack
snow, worn through
at the knees like acid-wash

denim. The grass beneath not frozen,
not killed, but insulated,
watered. Today, I dismantled

tree-forts in the woods, turned
trembling-aspen tent-poles
into nurse-logs. The goddamn-

everywhere moss so
green it made
my teeth hurt. *Frog-SONG!*

The winter's worth of sticky notes
the moose left around the yard

prove hard to ignore. I read

the ground around the shrub
rose I planted last spring before
I kneel & find more.

Stepped on & broken,
the rose looks rough but alive.
What's a thousand pounds

give or take? I'll have to take
the rose almost to the ground
if I want it to come back.

Went bushwhacking
with my friend the butterfly fiend.
He held the branches—the yellow-green

of new willow,
the red of last year's dogwood—
while I ran ahead, cutting here

& there. We crashed through
winter-stiff branches
companionably. He stopped

me when his fingers couldn't close
around our bundle. At home,
busy, I stuffed it

in a vase, where
it became a bedroom shrub instead
of basketry, a tension tray.

Today, reading
in bed, snow howling outside:
greening dogwood buds.

The house is more exposed
this spring thanks to moose.
Moose love dogwood most.

Had I known I wouldn't have
planted dogwood at all.
Perhaps I would have

planted more. The branch
ends, pruned & blunt,
talk back to the reach

& wrap of a thick tongue,
the drawing in pre-teeth
clench, pre-sideways tug

I came to know when I moved
back. There were no moose
in these parts when I was young.

I went for a walk under the
naked trees in a sweatshirt
& a light scarf, relying

on internal combustion
to keep me warm. I could
feel April all over the apples

of my withered cheeks
& the dogshit ground froze
around the feet of the person

who came before me. We
HONK-ed at geese standing
guard on the train bridge

for something to do.
Wednesday, I get
my first dose. *Whee!*

A jackrabbit sits
mid-drift
its fur

the colour of shadows
caraganas throw across
the puckered snow.

Five young deer
in the new grass on the green
of the decommissioned golf course,

five does in the cold shadows
behind. One un-antlered yearling
leaps on another's back

& goes limp. It's dragged
ten feet like a bearskin rug
or a deerskin coat, fresh

from the sewing
machine, ready for beading.
The deer shrugs the other off,

then they rise up like dancers
rehearsing or Rock 'em Sock 'em
fighters, bored & stiff.

The blackbirds, still here,
look down on me
& my language,

the shears I hold,
& the sage I hacked
as it catches a gust, tumbles

with goldenrod heads

into the chokecherry bush.
"So?" Hundreds of eyes

like chia seeds
in my easy overnight oats
watch me puff.

Midnight. Someone has posted a pic
of the spiky bleach-blonde head
of wild cucumber

to Native Plants of Manitoba,
intrigued, wanting to plant it
on their property. Someone replies:

"Watch out! It's invasive!"
Someone else: "Burn it!"
But wild cucumber *is* native to this place,

thriving in floodwater, climbing trees
& shrubs for goddamn millennia.
I realize—she means

prolific, resist the urge
to correct, language
like a burr in my cuffs,

hauled from place to place.

33

The north wind,
the all night, all day
relentless wind

winds me up. Is that me
yelling about money?
It blows so hard

the downspouts rattle
in the metal bands
holding them to the wall,

clatter like cutlery
in the hands of a child
taking forever

to empty the dishwasher.
Knife. Knife. Forks. Spoon.
The quality tinny.

I meet the fiend-friend for a walk.
Emboldened by vaccines, we follow
rabbits making short

work of new shoots
on the edges of sidewalks around
his house. Aching,

exhausted, we lean up

34

against my car like it was a blind
to watch a wood duck

roost on a chimney. The air warm,
the bowl of the horizon broken
& filled with gold. Drive home

like a granny so I can ogle a line
of geese, breaking & reforming

in the greying sky.

Smoke well south of here
this morning, closer smoke
north of here later & now

I move window to window,
our house a lookout tower
after fire took the barnyard last year.

We snuffed hotspots for days,
put down pails of water to wave
at rubberneckers. Had the wind turned

we would have burned alive,
our house a crockpot.
My chest hurt for ages, my heart

a charred chunk of timber. Fingers pointed

out bad wiring. Now black-
birds fly like ash over the roof.

Mid-afternoon, we go hunting
prairie crocuses. At the treeline, trembling
aspens draped with prayer flags

drop grey exhalations, catkins
past their prime. Dogs in the underbrush.
The air smells of rain

& the meadow is full of rosehips
& the silver leaves of artemisia. I rake
the long grass with my eyes

but only find crocuses in a protected
spot under rocks. I lie in the grassy pocket
beside them. I lie.

Rain barrel set-up halts.
Mice have chewed a hole
through the overflow hose.

A way to pass the winter,
I suppose. Maybe they needed
more roughage in their diet.

Maybe they hate us, our cats,

our live-traps, our dogged
attempts to grow leafy greens.

Maybe they had a leak
loaded with hantavirus. If so
it's airborne now. Squeak.

I said nothing when the Winnipeg
Mycological Society FB group murmured
It's too cold for morels

from the bedside table I inherited
from my mean Scottish grandfather.
My Irish great-grandfather

studied rodents, had mouse pelts posted
to him by friends. (Some friends!)
He was a splitter & eventually

proved wrong by science.
Last night, my partner swore
they planted a tree across the street,

but it was only a watering truck
servicing an existing tree.
Having learned my bedside manner

from my scientist mother,
who wore a lab coat but also heels,

I kept my trap shut.

Full moon. Cottonwood.
A great horned owl
calling from the slough.

Frogs singing all through
the hollow. A robin sounds
alarmed. Geese start up.

Grass rustles. Then nothing.
Standard crime novel stuff.
The sun has set. My old bones

have turned the mean
platelet volume way down.
I'm standing on the deck.

I'm standing on top of a fill hill
in the decommissioned golf course
toeing the licked lip

of an old jug, pearlescent
in the mud. I look through
it like it was a hagstone

& my favourite stand of conifers.
was a disguised coven of witches,

like it was a porthole

& the wind-blown boughs
a rough & changeable sea.
I look for fossils

in the limestone chunks & bits
of crockery with insignia
in the dirt

but mostly find
a full belly's worth of plastic
& bits of eggshell with albumen,

the inevitable mating pair
HONK-ing from the rough.

A mourning dove hunkers
in a hunch of dead grass
behind the house.

The odd coo registers.
The wind is something else.
It feels like the end

stop was destined to be
right here. Snowmelt trickles
near the dove's pale breast.

It sees me at the window.
It tilts its head giving light
to a pale orbital ring.

The quad is full of geese, prepping
for stump speeches, nibbling new blades
of grass. Others get in formation

on the rooftop, *HONK*-ing at the bent
necks of exhaust pipes, telescopes
& experimental beehives. I avoid them,

just like bottleneck pamphleteers
or people who stuff my mailbox with offers
to buy my house in their neatest

handwriting. I am nearly inside when I look
up & see two geese assholes lined
up over the roof's edge. *Bull's eye!*

Moose prints, wrist deep
in places, but mostly not
visible at all. A sinking

feeling now & then
with long stretches
of nothing but raspberry

canes with new twists
of leaves about
to spring. Moose,

this garden is yours.
This path is yours. This fence,
what's left of it, is a joke.

Drone everywhere, traffic, airplane
but I am dragged to the edge
of a cattail-choked

water-hazard
by a moaning men's choir
of wood frogs & boreal chorus frogs.

Have you ever clucked
like a chicken?
Have you ever stroked

the teeth of a comb?
I stand in the behead
seedheads of cattails, last year's

leaves gone blonde,
feeling both fucked
& clean, my eyes closed.

An influx of yellow-rumped
warblers scatter as I drag
my rump to the house,

the trip to town hounding me
already. Will I dream tonight
of birds flycatching or the flies

of the three guys, men
unmasked & manspreading
while standing up

near the only entrance of
the vaccination clinic?

A mudlarker posts a picture
of her riverbank handful: yellow shafts
of Northern flicker feathers, somehow

electric- AND candle-light.
I have not been outside, except
to play tennis, wind-whipped, cold.

Red-winged blackbirds sing backup
to the front-end loader dump,
the whine of hydraulics,

the post-vax head thump.

I think I'm going to die.
"I'm good with that," I say

to the only one in earshot.
Another load of dirt
arrives & rejoins the earth

with a humph, *with hints of spring*
melt, grouse feather, & I believe
the leavings of a skunk.

We have stepped off the dirt path
at Bois des Esprits to avoid
a foursome coming right for us,

when M stage-whispers:
"TURTLES." And everyone looks
towards the brown-green waters

of the Seine. One woman
steps into the riverside grasses,
then pauses: "Wait,

have you seen any snakes?"
"Oh yes," M says, smiling big.
"Garter snakes."

Her white sneakers flash like WTD
in retreat. I take shallow

breaths, noticing how the painted

turtles, stacked like bowls
in a drying rack,
ignore us completely,

how they bask.

Couch grass sews
the shrub border together
with shallow runners

& knots the roots.
Noxious weed meets
obnoxious yanker.

I sink the edger in after
to enhance the curve
to lead the eye somewhere.

I learned this from a book.
Lead where though? A robin
finds a worm in my pursuits.

The toothy bottom jaw
of a young deer in the brown
aspen leaves, the bone

& enamel falling somewhere
between tea & caramel. The other half
gleams whitely on a bed

of moss a few feet away. "Coyotes?" M asks,
referring to the warnings tacked up
at the park entrance, the jangly

headlines in the evening news.
I shrug, admiring its molars
& premolars, knowing

that I couldn't distinguish
between doe legs & trembling
aspens on a good day.

The garden, partly
planted ahead of the rain
that never came,

looks neat at least
with lengths of twine
tight as guitar strings

running east-west above
wind-smoothed dust,
strings plucked by deer

while I dreamed water.

Today a whirlwind
passed by the well.

"It might be too windy
for butterflies," fiend-friend says,
but we see

three mourning cloaks,
mudpuddling
on the limestone path. I spot

mushrooms like broken dinner plates
on old willows & wade in.
A wood frog, still

half-frozen, jumps half-heartedly,
hoping he's hidden
in the aspen mulch.

As I emerge from the brush,
my friend intones: "Watch out for the tree
monster." I scan

the horizon, pick winter-brittle
twigs from my hair & bark
from my bra

& realize he means me.

There's ice in the birdbath,
typical for an atypical spring.
The low pressure system

over Montana promises
needed moisture. The radar shows
the northeasterly flow will miss us.

Still the wind. Mood swings.
In the feeder a rose-breasted grosbeak
splits seeds alone, stares

me down, the rose blooming
in a puff of white. A snowfall
warning has been issued.

All week we waited for rain.
Pulmonaria bloomed bee-pink,
then inky-purple.

I will rip flowering
handfuls out later, when it tries
to take over. Groundcover? More

like groundsmother. It's the day
before May-long lockdown.
I am playing tennis when it starts

to rain. So I gather handfuls

of dandelions from a unused
baseball diamond, yellow running

the bases. I swear, I will stay
home all week if it keeps raining.
(Cankerworms float

down from the trees.)

Heat wave during the third wave.
The vulture circling my rocking chair
looks rough, some flight

feathers missing, some askew,
others holey & torn.
It's been that kind of June

& we're only four days in.
It seems I too have a molt sequence
that requires more study.

The vulture shifts its circle
east over the hollow, descends,
then rises again. I'm not fooled.

The sun sets into the house.
Plus 35 C outside, 27 inside.
We retreat to our bedrooms, window

air conditioners whirring. I heard
the city has turned on
the splash pads.

The only time I went out today
was to retrieve tomato seedlings,
growing in take-out

coffee cups, left on my steps
by a friend. They're wilted & I feel
a spasm of guilt.

Guilt is hot. I go sit
under the ceiling fan & gnaw
on frozen grapes.

Afternoon thunderstorm,
a sprinkling of hail
& now a halo.

Down with the shovel,
down with the trowel,
we run for the clearing.

I fall to my knees, camera
ready, as he turns & extends
both arms, palms upward

& outward in the ta da

here's our whole world pose,
here's our icy atmosphere.

Something yellow
warbles at me from a power line
on the other side

of this borrowed lakeside garden,
staked & stringed up.
Watering to pay for my bed,

I'm dragging hose around. It sounds
like it's being strangled,
but beautifully. Waiting for

a diagnosis: HPV? Cervical cancer?
Hummingbirds line up
along the porch rail. A dog barks

& barks across the road.
I steep myself in the lake, wretched
teabag.

We're both brackish.

Thirty paces from the garden
to the hollow & I'm back
among the anemones

I hadn't known were here
until yesterday when H said "Come
I have something to show you."

& with my best sigh I followed him
to the cottonwoods, happy
for the shush of leaves, the chance of shade.

I watch my step, not wanting to crush
even one. My wildflower book says
their petals are really sepals.

More like white yachts moored
to yellow docks.
I bend down like a god to look

upon a little fly swimming in raindrops
in the deep end of one.

My friend confided
there's an electronic fence
confining the yappy

dog. I audition rectangles.
Given the lake, the windy
shoreline, a rotten cervix,

a dubious attitude: trapezoid?
Rhombus? (The highway

killed the neighbour's

previous dog.) The poor soil kills
my friend's conifers,
though they've terraced their yard

with trees. My favourites? Hot-tub
 silver maple, outside-shower
silver maple & the scrubby thing

the hummingbirds
hide in between feedings.

With a hankering for saskatoons
we walk south to the coulee
pails in hand, go the long way around

avoid stepping in the field
between our place
& the unbroken prairie

to avoid spreading disease
from our shoes to the crop.
The coulee seems deeper this year,

the fringe of bushes
on the east slope near bare of berries,
the few small & blemished.

Toppled bushes reveal
a mop of roots
still connected to live suckers.

A head of tangled roots
in my sewer outflow, my dark hair
in the shower drain.

42 mm of rain
for all of June. I had that
on my basement floor last week,

except full of floaters. Premature
crops, bone-dry forests, fire
everywhere. It started

to rain as the Roto Router truck
pulled up. I stood on
the sidewalk,

my stomach / the sky
gently rumbling. Oh my thirsty
elm, my dirty hair.

Drought cracks my garden.
A grackle with grasshoppers
stuffed in its bill

flies toward the rising
noise of a well-hidden nest
then makes a return trip.

Creeping a farmer's tweets,
I learn this plague
stopped eating pasture yesterday

within minutes of being sprayed
How long until livestock
can safely resume grazing?

Parched & dying,
they'll cling to blades for days,
easy prey

when the bill inevitably comes.
Do they see the opening,
the pink tip of a nestling's tongue?

Wildfire smoke drifts in
& Environment Canada
takes a break

from extreme heat warnings
to issue an air quality
statement—elevated pollution levels,

but we stroll anyways, spotting

54

an octet of dead oaks
in my favourite boulevard

grove. The arborist who tested my elm
for DED said they're calling
it sudden oak death syndrome:

too many years of drought
pushing hardy trees
down the death spiral. In the smoke,

the sun burns red
& redder. And then, Oh god,
it rains.

For 63 years the Case has been working here
if I hear right over the idling diesel.
Dad is teaching H how to cultivate

the fire guard separating our yards
from crops & pastures
burning up in this drought.

Kept worked, that strip of dirt
might help us get out alive
should a bearing get too hot

at harvest. They stop & start
pulling bunched-up clover

away from the shovels

then crawl back on the tractor. The steel
seat sinks with weight. H drives.
Dad hangs onto the seat & fender.

My dirty little Prius
is dying. The air-conditioning
quit & it wheezes when

I step on the gas.
If the Widowmaker or worse
my beloved boulevard elm

fails, dropping on my car,
do I get a double payout
or just a double whammy?

Is this hurry up
& wait decline what I deserve
as a gas-guzzler? A city-dweller?

(Reports from friends
of coming home to tagged trees...)

Young partridge, about fifteen,
stick close to the adults
in the potato aisle,

a happy family it seems.
One stops then springs
over the very dirt

I sunk a fork into yesterday
accidentally stabbing
the best potato in the hill

which I then kicked off the tines
& threw in the pail. Norland,
worm-free & sweet,

might be the reason
I moved back here. Fresh baby
potatoes & butter until I die.

The partridge picks another
grasshopper off the potato plant.
They're on special this week.

We visited the ruins
of a glass factory in Beausejour.
On the trail in, glass sparkled in the dirt,

& then I found the giant heap
of purple slag, all lips
& mouths of bottles, all melted

by a bonfire or maybe a hundred years

of sun. We stopped to stare
at the water

in the silica sandpit next door, cheerfully
ignoring the *No Trespassing* sign
to have our lunch

while a rich woman walks the length
of the beach to tell us we had
to go. I had leftover pizza

but I would have much preferred to eat
the rich, nestled on the shores
of their private pit.

Listen. The cheers
of five barn swallow nestlings
as an adult swoops in,

lands on the nest's mud lip,
mud I made
near the edge of garden

with dribbles from the hose
so they could stick it to the house,
a trick I learned from the neighbour.

It takes a spillage to raise a wild
bird in a drought. If it means a mess

oh well. Has it ever been this dry

here? The swallow flies off
toward the crows feasting
in the field of lentils across the road.

Eat while you can, my friends.
I hear it's time to desiccate.
The sprayer will be coming soon.

Before the grass crunched, dry above
& glassy below, glassblowers
panting all over the landscape,

there was a yellow-green
cottonwood leaf on the gravel-studded
asphalt path. A nodule

where the stem attached
to the leaf. I like ruins
but as a lover

of trees, I was saddened
to find another way for trees
& shrubs to fail. Oak, willow,

wild rose & now, poplar galls.
Apparently this package
is stuffed full of aphids.

Through the door's bevelled glass
I see all five young swallows
perching on the half-cup, full

it seems & stretching wings
like they just got up. They look
as rested as I feel this morning.

Were they confused too

by the cool rain & wind,
at 4 am, the approaching rumble,
the cat meowing on the roof. I wonder

how long he's been stuck up there,
& how well a mud nest sticks
to vinyl when it gets wet?

Early to an outdoor meeting
at Vimy Ridge Park, I rested
my wilting July eyes

in the lushness of the community
garden, built on the defunct
lawn bowling green. Weeks ago,

I spent a socially-distanced hour,
shovelling mulch into the rows
of raised beds.

It looked like a coffin BOGO,
a row of sturdy plague ships, but now,
squash vines trail

on the drought-cracked sod,
potato greens are dying back
& it is BEAN SEASON.

Our meeting is cut short
by rain. About time!

Grasshoppers on shoulders
of grasshoppers. The place
packed. I'm in the first row.

Three rows of beans to go.
I reach between pairs,
come away with a bean

without snapping it,
drop it in the pail. A hero
never picks a fight

but I want enough
for the freezer, dammit.
Come on. Dismount already.

Vacation. My mother-in-law sends pics

of the sturdy hips of beets
pulled from garden boxes.

Her tomatoes—my friend's seedlings,
transplanted from my porch
to her pots—are perky

but she tells me she's dumping
water on them twice a day. We've asked her
to drive across the city twice

a day to feed our cats
as we drive across the prairies,
but today the air

quality health index
is bad, the smoky sky high-risk.
I urge her to stay

inside. At night, unventilated, I listen
to my lungs's parting curtains.
I want to go home

so I can walk across
the drought-emptied Assiniboine
without getting the tops

of my feet wet.

I find a shallow depression
the size of a large jackrabbit
north of the garden

in a spot I generally ignore.
The cat sniffs the dirt & rolls
in it as a vehicle goes by,

the dust drifting my way
as it generally does. We said no thanks
to the offered dust control applications

of calcium chloride or the like,
go instead with the house dressing.
It's more our price.

There's the rabbit now
heading straight for the lettuce.
Whoa! It hits the brakes hard,

waits ears straight up & out.
From the raspberry patch
comes the other cat, orange

tail flicking as it walks away.
Next time. The rabbit stretches.
The dust has not yet settled.

I feel hare-brained.

If I was a tree, I'd be heat-stressed,
dropping leaves. If I was a ham,

I'd be smoked. Friends mutter
about fourth waves
while governments drop mask

mandates & capacity limits. Me?
I can't separate aphid honeydew
from humidexed afternoons,

wildfire smoke from
respiratory droplets. *Cough cough.*
It's so droughty, so dry

I've taken to watering
my old elm, despite roots
breaking into my weeping tile

like it was backyard shed
full of bikes. (Later, my friend confides
the city charged the community garden

$1200 for water. Part of me
wants to know: how much

is that per tomato?)

The goldenrod takes gold

in the floor routine.
I am floored

by how much it has spread
in spite of the drought.
Everything else is suffering.

Crickets cricket at my feet,
cricket in the pasture
where a cow lets out a moo.

A sad moo. No bull this year.
The cow is a cull soon
headed to market. I think

it knows. The herd of culls
grazes, their calves sucking,
bunting. The cows look tired.

The pasture looks tired.
I am too. I want the gold
to mean something.

I want it all to mean
something, the flooding/drought
of end times. On the mountain

yesterday, we heard people
yipping like coyotes, the landscape

otherwise empty,

& noticed how pristine
our windshield was. Time
was, a drive across

the prairies meant a wriggling
horizon of horror.
Strange, but I miss it. I miss

July thunderstorms like
a diminishing aunt
I haven't seen in two years.

*Nothing makes us laugh
like the forecast: 30 percent
chance of showers.*

*Risk of a thunderstorm. Right!
It's mostly sunny. Smoky. Smunny.
The reflection annoying: Who*

*threw the can on the road?
No one litters nowadays
on backroads in these parts.*

*It means a stranger passed by
as we slept. Out enjoying the stars?
Looking for hay? Good luck.*

I'm told it's a Coors can.
There's another halfway to town.
"And you just left them there?"

I say. "That's money!" We laugh.
I stare at the can, picture the glowing
butt of a smoke falling next.

I left my toothbrush
on the vanity. The day before
we left, I dropped

plans to walk the Lemay Forest,
a riverbottom forest
hidden in one of the Red's deep

curves, apparently studded
with milkweed. Instead,
I check the Save the Lemay Forest

FB group from Calgary,
find bald men posting telephoto pics
of eagles & grosbeaks, the velvet

antlers of bucks. Developers want
to put in a nursing home.
Every time someone says: "We'll save

the next one!" I want to ask:

will we recognize ourselves,
or the city, in twenty years?

The old stars
seem more reachable
the longer I look,

though harder to see
tonight with the smoke.
Last night, with zero gravity

chairs fully reclined, I said
"This might be the last time
we see meteors. What if

fire season never ends? What if
a supervolcano lets go? What if
a moose comes along

& doesn't notice us sitting
on its path? What if we close
our eyes to everything?"

Between Horseshoe Canyon
& Drumheller, between the car
& the roadside fields,

full of knee-high grains

& freshly baled hay, between local-
smoke & gravel-road

kick-up, we finally got
yellow smears on the windshield.
Not that I liked running down

insects at speed,
but it meant they were present.
That I was moving through

the landscape instead of treating it
like a research project,
cataloguing the effects

of wildfire smoke on wildlife,
staying up late reading papers
on the lungs

of polo horses,
"uniformly inflamed" with intra-
cellular debris & pollen,

having manufactured full-blown
asthma after

weeks of smoke.

August night bugs come through

69

the screen & beat themselves
up on the wall above the light.

I turn off the lamp & the bugs
beat my phone, my eyes,
my patient side.

Will they head for the green light
on the smoke detector again
& set it off?

They find ways to get in my ears.
I pull the sheet over my head
& the bugs sound like raindrops.

This morning, people pulled
sweaters out of storage
to wait at the brunch place,

but it refused to rain. On the yellowing
slope of Nose Hill
we met my childhood pen pal,

pausing in shoals of old aspens,
admiring just-opened wild
roses & fading blanket flowers

along the trails. In the parking lot,
a few drops of the rain

on my face. Surely,

it rained *somewhere*.

A quick trip to town
to pick up four bags of flour
they put away for us. On sale.

Anyone who knows crops
& what failure means
is stocking up. Along the way

we see thin cows hanging close
to water tubs where water
tubs have never been before.

The clouds spit a few times.
I feel as low as the water level
in our well. A well we share.

We start out, the sky open—
purest blue, whitest white,
the foothills bundled in rough

cloth. We use dark clouds
as landmarks, the skyline smudged:
a slough, a weather-beaten

fence, brown cows. We watch
goldenrod & silvery artemisia sway,
until rain pounds

the windshield, like grain falling
into an elevator, like clods
of earth from a shovel.

Mineral damp invades the car.
I watch a big tree in the middle
of a pasture forever.

We drive in & out of rain.

The farmers no longer joke
about a crescent wrench
dropped in a drought crack,

but the whole toolbox
banging the sides on the way
down. I wake with a jolt. Look out.

On the gravel path to the house
an immature house wren is bathing
in a puddle for the first time.

A friend in Winnipeg reports
she left a water glass outside & came out

this morning to find it

half full. People *wahoo*,
post pictures of wet sidewalks but
the news says it came too late

for farmers, at least in Manitoba. We park
under my boulevard elm,
unload our bags, then hurry

to the farmer's market
for our regularly-scheduled
CSA veg pick-up.

Over the bin of extra-cukes,
the friendly-neighbourhood-farmer
shrugs, says he only got a half inch.

Before going in, I force myself to check
my elm: no orange blot yet.
Later, we sit on the couch

with the door open
& listen to rain.

Two tenths. That's all
the rain we got yesterday.
Today a mean northwest wind

puts us back where we were.
Too windy to work close
to old maples

thrashing limbs at 75 km per hour,
we drive up the road to visit
the neighbours who lead us

to the corn patch & load our arms
with ears. The corn,
waving brown silks, is ready

going by the cobs cleaned off
by a raccoon overnight. The leaves
tsk tsk.

"A million leaves on a mature elm," says
A Natural History of North American Trees.
But I somehow spotted

two flagging branches
near the street, where I park my car
if I'm lucky. Our neighbours have a pair

of standard poodles that need
to be driven to the dog park.
Our neighbours have a motorcycle, draped

like a grand piano. There's a yoga studio

at one end of the street, an elementary school
at the other. My block is busy

losing trees. "Six weeks
for the results," said the arborist, making
eye contact over his mask.

Jackrabbit
eye aimed at the clear blue sky.
Lying on its side,

feet against the bottom step.
As far as the cat dragged it,
an unsettling feat given that

every way is uphill & the prey
bigger than the predator.
A scientist

on Twitter schooling about
cats roaming free killing birds
& another talking back

about rodent control. I know
the arguments & respect
the science. And yet. The cat licks

his bloody ruff as he's been doing
here for years

75

Siteseeing • Ariel Gordon & Brenda Schmidt

before we showed up.

Walking to a vacant-lot
beer-garden, towards
the butternut tree on the next block.

But first, I stop on the boulevard
to show M. "I can't see it," he says.
"Come stand by me," I say, then raise

my arm to point: another branch
of my boulevard elm gone
crispy. We stare up

into the canopy. "What kind of tree
should we get to replace it? " he asks.
I shake my head, start walking.

A block away, every elm encircled
with orange ribbon: Every Child Matters.
A block away, every butternut

carefully gathered,
the ground bare: What could I—

what could we have done differently?

Grasshoppers jump off tomatoes

& land on the remains of beans
as I show the neighbour what's left

of my garden, ask for advice
& mirror the posture, the cool gaze.
They're eating the trees too.

Haskap leaves, gooseberry leaves,
the gooseberries themselves,
leaves of old caraganas & new

dogwoods, potentillas, elders,
all the diversity & potential
I had planned for the yard

growing bare, some near dead
from drought, heat, & now this
hunger, fall growing near. Shrug.

The fiend-friend wants to walk
in the forest in the hottest
part of a heatwaved Sunday.

35 C. Piles of dropped leaves
under cottonwoods & the caraganas
have gone yellow-green. We haunt

the limestone paths, the native
wildflower beds, the corridors of common

milkweed: a few cheap-and-cheerful

cabbage whites
& an eastern tailed blue,
where there should be a sky-full of things,

fluttering. We resort to
fields drowning in invasive
thistle & find five just-emerged monarchs,

the sun shining through them
like fire, like the time I put a flashlight
in my mouth

& thumbed it on.
Then we spot the yellow panties
of an orange sulphur in a thistle

& Elmer-Fudd it over,
only to realize that it's dead.
We still take photos. On the way out,

we empty our water bottles
into our mouths, waggle heat-swollen
fingers like none of this belongs to us.

In the shade of the spruce
five hummingbirds fight for position
at the feeder. Little socialists

they are not, clearly striving
to drive their pointy bills
into the brains of opponents.

Mom & I laugh & laugh
as two hummingbirds
face off & buzz straight up

into the clouds. We lose
sight of them until they buzz
their way back.

It's angry-wasp August,
black & yellow assholes
hovering at my elbow, attempting

my open mouth. We lost
a month of summer to wildfires & drought.
The forecast said there was

a 100% chance of rain. It's pissing
now, but the forecast
confirms: it's too late

for farmers, even as I collect dainty
zucchini at the farmer's market,
wasps licking

everyone's ice cream.

Last night, I bled through
my new buttercup linen-blend

pants at the lawn-chair shiva
for my friend's mother, darkness
a sweater wrapped

around my matronly hips. *Siiiiiiiigh*.
What if my enthusiasm
for the world

is misplaced?

30 mm last we looked.
Neither one of us emptied
the rain gauge. We just couldn't.

170 mm more & the soil,
a slow-mo shattering plate,
might hold enough

perhaps to grow a crop
next year, maybe, says some
hydrologist, if I remember right.

Remembering is hard now. I stare
out the window, flinch & duck
as a slow-flapping bulk of grace

clears the house, its underside
grey as the clouds. The heron
follows the curves of the slough

& sets down at the dugout.
I'm sure
there's some water there.

We've had days of rain now & according
to my local mushroom FB group,
oysters

& boletes are flushing
but I am spending
the morning in my car in a busy

vet parking lot, waiting
for my sick cat. No diagnosis for my elm
either. I am trying to stop

humming the tune that goes
unhappy-unhappy-
dead-yellow leaves-dropped

leaves-dead-
dying as I drive through
the city, to keep my eyes from rising

into the trees. In the news,

a driver with a display home
on his trailer

at 5 am, who knocked down
or chainsawed 23 mature trees
on the median. I try

to imagine panicking

with a chainsaw.

Some days I don't need to hide at all,
that's how isolated we are,
but I do today

behind the fence
we built with cow-smoothed fir
reclaimed & repurposed

to conceal the Adirondack.
It has my back
as it has for more than 30 years.

Here the morning glory is more purple
prose turning to emphatic fuchsia
near the middle. The white throat

practically glows. I'm weak,
simply put, for whatever reason.

More blooms tomorrow.

A week of rain. Worm jerky
& flattened grasshoppers on the blue
courts, pelicans soaring whitely

above. The middle distance full
of yellow wasps, buzzing our faces
& inner arms. All my balls wind up

in other people's courts. We sweat
& swat. I languidly return
a too-long serve & knock a wasp

out of the air. Later, walking Bunn's Creek,
someone has knocked down a nest,
the gray football leaking weak

& disoriented wasps.
I pocket the three pages of paper
that was their roof, built

out of fences & windowsills.
Next week, school starts.

September already?
I trim the maples & choke-
cherries with shears which feels wrong

in a drought. All that
hard-won growth for not. I hack
away at the caragana next, manage

only to scuff its bark. Cranes
croak high overhead as I call H
for the chainsaw. It bites & binds

halfway through. I'm not holding
the branch taut enough.
"Try again," I say, trying not to

look up. The branch lets go.
Seed pods, empty & twisted,
clap away.

I've been diving in & out
of Assiniboine Forest like it was a pool
& I was retrieving weights

on its bottom. Surfacing with my hands
full of the deep orange caps
& scabrous

stems of birch boletes, coral
mushrooms candelabra-ing on wet logs.
After spotting shaggy

scalycap clustered at the base

of aspens, fiend confesses
he's into mushrooms now,

like he's cheating with my boyfriend.
I call him into the woods, saying "I saw
a brown butterfly!"

but he shakes his head, like he doesn't
believe me.

I've been alive so long
call or click-before-you-dig
used to be dial.

At the click of the handheld
detector they stoop to stick
a metal stake in the ground

in front of the western
snowberry we transplanted
this summer. In the wind

the rectangular red plastic
flag flaps the words
SaskPower.

Three black arrows
point to exactly where
I tend to stand with the water.

85

Today I caught the hind-
& fore-leg of a painted lady hunkered
down in a fuschia

zinnia with my aging
cellphone. Tack-sharp, it ignored me,
feeding amongst the disc florets. I forwarded

the butterfly to fiend.
In Omand's Creek, the compound
eyes of an upended grocery cart, covered

by an inch of blue-grey water.
The boulevards flushed
with clumps of mushrooms, a legacy

of left-over elm roots, above-ground
growth gone. I am planning a winter
of drought-tofu

& legumes, stocking a climate-changed
pantry, meat galloping
out of my reach.

Meanwhile, I'm seeding
 clouds with thoughts of rain.

"The well is down to the eighth ring,"
H says as I water in the lily bulbs

we bought from the buy & sell.

I want to see what he means but I can't
bring myself to lower my eyes
nor do I have the strength

to haul them back up without
thinking of the farmer down the road
found dead in the well he was digging

by hand before my time. Story goes
his glasses stayed at the bottom
when the hole was filled in. Later

when my family farmed that land
I'd rummage through the ruins of his home.
"What is the eighth circle again?"

I ask thinking of the divine comedy
we call retirement. Wire rimmed?
"Ring," H says. "Ring."

I have been storing the gold
of fall sunshine in my hair & the eyes
I inherited

from my father. Last week,
I made a triptych of spore prints
from an orange rosette

of velvet foot mushrooms,
growing on an elm stump, white spores
on black paper.

Last week, the mushroom guy
at the farmer's market announced
on IG he was voting

for the far-right People's Party of Canada,
which advocates pulling out
of the Paris Climate Accords.

I peer at his piles
of lion's manes from a distance now,
feeling black & white. No news

yet about my tree.

Weird.
The pair of livestock guard dogs
appeared on Tuesday morning.

The soft white giants looked
more magical than anything,
long tongues slung

over canines as they settled
on the hill for a spell,
waiting, I think, for me

to go away. One made eye contact
as I stood among the maple bugs,
the other scanned the herd of cattle,

the faint rust stain on its chest
the blood of coyote, I suspect,
from another day. Half-hidden

by the gold leaves of cottonwood,
I watched them leave. Shakespeare's
witches have nothing on me.

I laid under my boulevard elm
this morning, flattening
the unmowed grass

like a deer. The cats yelled
at me from the screened-in porch
but there it was: the flagging

limb, first bare of leaves
now bare of bark too. The tree
on the other side

of the street, its overhanging
branches an expressway
for squirrels but also disease-

carrying beetles with a taste

for deadwood. Without knowing it,
I carried

the elm's serrated leaves in
on the back of my shirt,
shedding them like feathers.

Sunday. I wake to gunfire.
Three shots from a high-powered
rifle west of the house.

I hold my breath.
Either it froze last night or I'm dead.
Lying on my back, cold, stiff,

I go with the latter. Who knows,
maybe it was a muzzleloader.
How many shots did it take

to make my brain wave
hello? Awareness
might be good right about now.

I wouldn't be the first to take
a stray bullet in bed. I wait
for the fourth. Hear starlings.

The trailhead of the pocket woods

near the Royal Canadian Mint has a sign
in the tarnished-yellow

shrub layer: *Private Property.*
No Fires or Loitering
Allowed Anywhere in the Wooded Area.

Though there are coins
jangling off the production line
on the other side of this accidental

treeline—trembling aspen suckering,
Manitoba maple volunteering,
cottonwood

towering—though there are likely
silvery coyotes waiting
in bushes & unsecured-garages

for twilight, all I can hear
is a man hallooing
for his lost dog. When we emerge

from the trees, he makes eye contact.
"Ladies," he says, "have you seen
a white dog?" We shrug.

The first snow is all about
celebration, letting go. Melting.

I hear the smooch of tires

stay out of sight,
unable to make myself wave.
Maybe tomorrow.

From the road allowance
spooked juncos by the hundreds
rise to the occasion.

The rumble of the diesel
fades & I'm left with the drip
of water on the step.

Yellow leaves fall.
A junco sets down in a puddle
& quickly bathes.

Morning. The horizon fogged,
rain coming. A garbage truck, painted
a garish green,

swallows paper bags
of leaves for composting-elsewhere,
groans hydraulically

hysterically as it attempts
the corner. Across the street, thirty geese
nibble the school field's

still-green October grass, forcing
teenagers to play frisbee golf around them,
metal chains rattling. A gull

soars the length of the field,
leaving me to drag
my mother-in-law's empty blue bin

up the driveway. I have come to mow
her rainbow chard, to pack
my freezer

with veg, cheerful survivalist.
I plan to pulverize
her remaining marigolds for ink.

October 16th:
two butterflies
probe gold gaillardia

as if they can't believe it either
while two two-striped
grasshoppers get it on

on the snow-in-summer (apt
name for a plant it seems)
two days after actual snow fell.

The snow is gone, the road

already dusting. Everything is so dry
right now. I rub dust off the lens,

take a pic. An expert
will later say they are common
checkered skippers & I

will love it & the algorithm
that places butterflies
in her feed.

We stalk the riverbank in shirtsleeves.
The mud criss-crossed
by raccoon & gull prints, the exposed

rocks studded with absurd
sequins of zebra mussels. I pull up
a broken blue & white plate

from the river, beaded with veligers
but missing the famous pair of birds.
The silty water clearer

the last few weeks, filter feeders busy.
Standing in the river, I pull out
my phone, follow invasive

red from the US border north
to the mouth

of the Hudson's Bay. Small suns

on the water, shoreline glinting
with shards of solarized
lavender & turquoise glass.

We are enclosed by trees & veins
of clay, homeless encampments
& pleasure craft.

We lose the light.

Redpolls pass crown to crown
from elm to maple to cottonwood,
none settling down,

tiny eyes measuring me
as I remove the dried
goldenrod, yarrow, rosebud,

& sunflowers from the band
of the witch hat H & I made
yesterday for something to do.

Two sheets of watercolor paper
became brim & cone
we then covered

with matte black fabric

once used as a backdrop
when photographing paintings

back in the days of slides.
Was I ever an artist?
Long lines of hot glue

hold it together. The hat
proved two sizes too small.
And now it's November.

I drive from aspen parkland
into boreal shield, from the grey-
green-white of trembling aspens

to the whitened teeth
of peeling birch, in a few hours.
It's like running into a cousin I haven't seen

in years, my father's features,
the family jokes, strangely
re-arranged. I don't even unpack

the car before stumbling out
under the Whiteshell's trees. It's somehow
9 degrees in November & the rocky

ground, the bark-split trees
studded with mushrooms.

I neeeeeeed a cup of tea.

Sunset. A truck goes by,
hits the brakes 150 yards away,
creeps ahead

angles north a bit to better see
the slough.
My inner action figure

nudges the front door open
with my knee hoping
the hunter won't notice.

The big camera & lens
steady my trembling hands.
Autofocus is my friend.

Deep breath. Quick clicks.
I am bold. A NO HUNTING *sign.*
The truck speeds off,

brakes at the top of the hill.
OK now I'm scared. Now off
it goes for real. I check my pics

see a clear enough image
of the driver's hand pointing
a rifle out the window.

First snow, mid-November.
I'm not sure what I'm more scared of
on my highway drives to work

this week: ruts filled with slush
or fall-back bucks
bounding

from the ditches: *Watch for deer*
for the next 11 km, the roadside
sign blares. Funny,

the Internet swears
my friend's husband is out
hunting somewhere in Saskatchewan,

but he gets the A-OK
from farmers first. He hangs
his deer from a hook in his garage

& breaks them down
to a pile of paper packages
in his chest freezer. I helped him once,

borrowing a one-piece
work-suit & a knife. He removed the head
before I arrived as a courtesy.

When we chow down
on venison & swill cava

at his annual BBQ, we joke

about the hook, call him Bluebeard,
serial killer. Other years, I intoned
"When the zombie apocalypse

comes, we'll FEAST
on super-abundant deer
& geese, at least for a while."

(This year's BBQ was cancelled.)

A rough-legged hawk hovers
as we slow down to watch,
its wings flapping like my jaw

when I attempt to say it out loud.
Its head bows to the northwest wind
in field guide fashion.

The truck hits the gravel ridge.
Five full water jugs clunk in the box.
17.8 litres each. It takes 124 litres

per month to meet our thirst.
To think I drank water from the well
for a year before we thought to test it.

Hi, high levels of nitrate! Am I blue?

Up ahead another rough sits
atop a quintessential shot-up curve sign

which reminds me: I text
my hunter brother about the buck
we saw standing by the road

at the top of Bone Coulee
on the way to town. It was missing
most of its right antler.

Six am. I see the silhouette
from a distance & slow
down to see a buck cross the road

from farmer's field to malt factory,
conjured by dawn, by hunting season
& rut. My friend's husband

swears deer can sense city limits
in the fall. I swear
there was frost on his antlers

but maybe I am projecting. I scan
the roadside for more deer
but that's a doe tactic.

Post-buck, two trucks
with snow plows bolted to the front

& two hundred meters of road,

then nothing but glittering
ice fog. The world contracts.
Irish Siri narrates:

3.2 kilometres to your destination.
I creep along.

*Half a maple down, half
a blizzard to go. Snow rear-ends
the house at 92 km per hour.*

*More than one neighbour
bets we'll lose power. One posts
a pic of a roadside billboard*

in the middle of a nearby nowhere.

*272 million in upgrades, it says.
Record-breaking investment
in rural infrastructure. SaskPower*

*getting old. Afraid of freezing,
our record breaking investment
sits under the deck ready to go.*

*Beside the generator a trap is set
for those who like wires. Rodents*

can't always help themselves.

Someone shares a picture
of 800 tightly-packed pronghorns
on the highway

near Maple Creek, SK
to Facebook. Someone else notes
the pic is a year old, dutiful

fact-checker. I peer at all the beige
pronghorn butts, the bluster
of the whitewashed

horizon & feel glad I avoided outside
entirely today, wind
shuffling around the house,

freezing rain falling
throughout the day. Everyone
else slipped on the ice so I didn't

have to. I might have hi-beam
nightmares about those pronghorns,
tomorrow's 6 am

drive in. On my way
upstairs with another cup
of milky tea, I tell M I love him.

From my pocket, Irish Siri
chimes in: *You are the wind
beneath my wings.*

*A covey of partridge crests
the drift & races to the bottom
like they're making fun*

*of my career prospects,
my body of work.
It's not like I always think*

covey *when I see them.
No one says* covey *here.*
Flock, *we say. The flock*

*squints as a unit as a gust
hits their bottoms, lifts feathers
all Marilyn Monroe.*

*They seem delighted
& commence scratching.
If I move they'll burst into flight.*

I come out of a long tunnel of work,
of overcast days, to sun. It spreads
over my face,

filling its cracked
drywall. I feel like a handyman
special, all string & duct tape,

leftover knob & tube. But the roads are bare
& dry & I don't have to think
about driving, I don't have to think

about black ice or visibility, the deep
ruts in the road. Beyond the perimeter,
the malt factory belching

beery exhaust, there's a flicker
of movement, corvids pecking
at what looks like a welcome mat

in the ditch, something brown
& ragged, lying unevenly
on the ground. It occurs to me

that it could be the buck
I passed & maybe someone else
picked it up like a spare

in a bowling alley, pins knocked down
at a semi-industrial 70 km per hour.

I am still unseasonable.

*"Chronic wasting disease ravaging deer
population near South Saskatchewan
River" says the CBC headline*

*the hunter posted earlier while waiting
in his blind. That's near here
where herds of starving deer resorted*

*to bales & trees last winter. Insurance
claim guidelines appear in my feed.
The news smells of a coming cull, some say.*

*The hunt concludes. The bare right
hand holds the base of the right antler,
the broken brow tine hiding the thumb.*

I ache all over, but don't line up
for a COVID-19 test. The news says
Omicron has migrated

to Hamilton, that COVID
has been logged
in Québécois WTD. M calls in sick,

then my daughter says she's feeling
sick too. I reverse-RVSP
for dim sum with friends,

a concert with another friend,

Sunday dinner with the in-laws.
In my feed, someone has captured

pics of a raptor
through a porch door
stripping feathers from a pigeon—

the snow pink, coated
in grey feathers, the raptor
sitting on its prey

like it was a throw pillow.
Flightless, I content myself
with low-res

after-the-fact accipiter
eye contact, the yellow sun

of that angry eye.

A bull moose
cuts through the sunrise
stopping now & then

to take in the humans
squabbling on the step.
H holds a hoodie out to me.

"Go away," I say. "How am I

supposed to put that on
& take pics at the same time?

You're wrecking my shot."
"Do you want frostbite?" he says.
"The steam is wrecking it for you,"

he adds. I close the door.
The moose hears the click,
raises his antlers & turns

to me & my nightgown. I hold
my breath. For a moment all is quiet,
freezing hide, sky yellow & lilac.

Our test results came through at 3:34 am:
negative. M & I, snoring a duet deep
in our duvet, missed it.

Later, the lymph nodes
under my chin swollen, he unearths
nighttime cold medicine

& brings it bedside. I protest,
but he tells me to cut the bull
& take it anyways. And I dry up

like a wrenched faucet. Our latest cat,
a fluffy formerly-feral ginger

that doesn't mind the cold,

demands his twenty wintry
minutes on the screened porch.
The police helicopter rattles

the picture frames while I flip laundry,
scrub the blasted asterisks
of byssal threads from a chunk

of Medalta crock, the spongeware rim
of a chamber pot. By spring,
I will be reconciled

to the blue carpet of zebra mussels
on my favourite curve
of the Red. I will have gumbo

protocols, separate rubbers
for each river & a jug of bleach
for washing up.

The cat wants out, so out
he goes, gallant with orange fur
in a kingdom of frost,

off to defend this place or die.
The cat comes back
like my post-booster headache

& behind him, a buck,
antlers sharp & tines
long enough,

The flu was last week's news
& it was unspeakably sunny, so I visited
the two highest places in Winnipeg:

the sixth floor of the Manitoba Clinic,
where all the preggers & peri-
menopausal women waddle off

the elevator. Every time I'm waiting
to hear that it isn't cervical,
uterine, or ovarian cancer, I lean

on the waiting room window, looking
for the exact spot
the city disappears

under trees. Afterwards, I chauffeur
my ladyparts to Garbage Hill,
an old landfill with a disposable sheet

of grass overtop, where gopher holes
leak milk glass & hotelware.
I apply myself to the muddy ridges

& Russian Olive-d slopes, learning

everything there is to know about weak
sun & strong wind, my hair tossed

like salad. Later, I crash
into bed like someone who has forgotten
the difference between gas

& brake, sick & well.

The same cube van speeds by
for the second time today,
as nondescript & predictable

as cube vans get. Heading east
this time. A hundred redpolls
lift from the hollow, bellies

cube van white. I wish
I could roll up that roll-up door
with my mind, imagine

the cargo. Hospital sheets,
plumbing supplies, a stainless
steel fridge with guarantee

of fingerprints, a mystery
tucked up front, coffee-stained
& dog-eared, straight out of a little library.

Redpolls aside, I'd say I'm witnessing
a crime. In these parts it's a crime
to not wave.

It's the Saturday before Xmas.
We should be out picking up bookstore
gift cards, parading our padded

selves on walking trails.
But we find ourselves gripped
by the desire to stay home.

The temperature is -21 C
with the windchill but the forecast
calls for 1,000 cases of Omicron

a day. My sister texts,
asking me to bring Brussels sprouts
for 14 to Xmas dinner next week:

Eeeeek!

Images of COVID, spikes & all,
made in the yard while I slept.
Two circles, each two deer lengths

in diameter & a herd apart,
each loaded with tracks,

not the usual dig marks,

but marks with certain lightness,
an elegance, a score perhaps,
an abundance of action

to guide the play of antlers
clattering under the moon
feet from my window. Encore!

This morning with a tweet
Environment Canada confirms
the presence of COVID-19

in a deer outside of Saskatoon.
I really hope the works of us live
to see the snow banksy melt.

There's no bad weather,
only bad people. I was supposed
to walk today but mid-day

my friend confessed
via pixelated screen: "Too cold
for this wimp." It's good he knew

to insult himself so I didn't have to.
Instead, I read about scientists
using machine learning

to predict which animals
are more likely to catch
COVID from us then pass it back,

which they called "spillback infections"
& "secondary spillover infections."
I scan the tables

like they're set
for Xmas dinner: cats & dogs
but not raccoons. White-tailed deer

& deer mice but not house mice.
Pigs & cows, cougars but not
big brown bats. I have

to say: I feel perforated

by the idea of an infected wild.

Tire tracks through fresh snow, off-road,
a single set heading around the old
yard site my family once owned.

A raven sat balloon-necked
on a poplar calling in reinforcements.
A bald eagle circled the yard

as we drove by. The clean-up crew

had arrived. But why? I passed along
my observations & news

of a missing person in the southeast.
"Long way to go to dump a body,
don't you think?" I was told. Later

I saw lights. Today the rumour
machine tells me they're looking
for helium. Noble & inert,

I take the news like I take all news
these days. One could say
I'm in my element.

At the river bank, a rodent
superhighway had been erected
overnight, with breathing holes

& burrows, just like Bugs
used to make through
my Albuquerque-d childhood.

We were trudging
through all that snowy buttercream
to the brewery, where the bank

is almost entirely glass,
when we spotted one of the ice

mice, fleeing.
It was good to see something
alive, to startle
over something small.

The snow light. My boots squeak
like a choir of mice, tenors mostly,
more baritone when I carry a shovelful.

Fifty sparrows chirp in the feeders.
Not sopranos. I let the snow fly
& the wind carries it halfway

to the garden where the winter interest,
as garden influencers put it, is ok, but
could be more lively. The sparrows

have grown quiet. Sunflowers tip
caps of snow for the win. I tip back,
squeak parka against cheek.

"Frostbite in minutes," the forecast
said. Going by my ears I'd say three
minutes out of the wind, less than

one in. A few more scoops & throws.
What I wouldn't give for a proper hood.

On Boxing Day, long lines

for free KN95 masks at Liquor Marts
& booster shots instead of flatscreens,

bins of tinsel & bows. Later, I walked
in the forest, snowpantsing
through deep snow,

childhood pen pal
in front of me on the path, wild
licorice to either side,

up to its sticky seedheads
in fresh powder. We stare into the entrails
of an old car near the fenceline

like it could help
us tell the future. "My dad would be able
to say exactly which model it is,"

she says, COVID having kept
her from her elderly parents
for 18 months. We swish

through a crossroads
& see a doe in the distance,
looking at us looking at her. I almost raise

my vaccine-sore arm to wave.

Extreme cold warning.

A bull elk grazing in the field
north of the house in the before-sunrise

noses 30 below stubble, snow,
lifts its head, chewing while looking
side to side, antlers held high,

then head back down, tines rocking
royal waves. It's too dark to capture
steam rising from its nostrils.

Heraclitus said you can't step
in the same river twice but M says
I shouldn't step in the winter river

AT ALL. But I've been intrigued
by the steaming water where there's
a sewer outflow

for weeks—it never freezes.
Waterfowl specialize
in those sites, while deer hoof-split

the bank before skittering
across semi-solid ice. Trudging along,
I get into a fist-fight

with still-standing common
burdock & emerge with spiky mitts,

117

huffing like a browsing
elk. I stop on the bank to stare
at four geese on a floe
in the centre of the flow, heads twisted

back & tucked between their wings.
I give them 30 feet before descending
to the bank on my bottom.

I promised M I wouldn't wade so I creep
the edge & get a booter
instead. I use the butt

of my new Japanese trowel
to collapse the overhanging edges,
watch them float away like puffs

of smoke in the gurgling water.
My glasses fog over & freeze
in the twilight. I can't see,

my scarf is damp & my foot is starting
to ache with cold. I call M
to come get me, proving

him right. He sucks his teeth

but doesn't say anything.

New Year's Eve day. Beyond cold.
Betty White has died.
A glass punch bowl set

posted minutes ago
on the local buy & sell for $25.
There's the spirit

growing exponentially.
Time to mop the condensation
off the windows.

Fog greys the horizon
from northeast to southwest over
the South Saskatchewan River

& the dam. There's a name
for the waves of snow
here on the hillside over which

a magpie steers its tail
& shadows sail north
to the cottonwood. I can't remember

anything. Another supply chain issue
makes the news. The fog is closing in.
I should step out just to say I did.

My one frostbitten resolution?

To spore-print looming
February afternoons, flush

my office with lion's mane
& black pearl king oysters, grow
kits in plastic tubs.

Around eight, I am swilling
grapefruit sparkling wine
& playing boardgames. My friend wins

every game but I'm drinking
her wine, so: I win? Midnight, I am in bed
but not asleep. Some people bang

pots when the clock ticks over,
but we tried to knock ourselves out
early. Morning & the extreme

windchill means that after picking up
the girl from her annual NYE sleepover
it will take hours

for my hands & feet to return
to room temp. My car
feels like a black bear roused

from hibernation before its time,
rocking & lumbering over ruts.

The shrike looks happy enough
sitting alone in the maple
sheltered from the wind,

no evidence of butchery
hanging from a V
where branch meets trunk,

no sparrow, no vole,
no mouse. Part of me
wants to post its prey online.

Frost on its black mask sparkles
as the shrike peers through the window,
stretches & yawns like it's waiting

for an order of wings,
wonders what's taking so long.
It opens & closes its bill once more,

a government
with the means to follow up,
wipes the hook on the bark. All done

without malice, after all, the goal
a tidy ending. A bird has to eat
the odd bird to keep going.

I spend the -37 degree day hiding

121

from the weather, sorting
hundred-year-old pieces of stained glass,

waste from middle-class
entry-ways, from the hey-day
of church windows. I own every colour

but have garbage hills
of green & blue: land & sky, leaves
& background. It's *almost* as good

as a button jar borrowed
from an old lady. Yesterday, sundogs
nipped at our plastic bumper

all the way home, my toes going
numb. Today, I risk
my tender fingertips, stirring

my shoebox of glass. I look out
at the snowy roof of the shed, overlaid
with shadows of trees & realize

that every shard on my desk
is me, bending over,

reaching for something.

It's my birthday. I want to go for a drive

so off we go, unload our recyclables
in the blue trailer on Main Street

in the once village, once hamlet,
now unincorporated community
where the old Co-op store,

now confectionery & restaurant,
reputed to have the best butter chicken around,
has no vehicles parked in front,

the lunch hour past. I want to take
the long way home, camera on my knee
ready for a herd of pronghorns, deer,

a snowy owl. We slow by the creek
where sometimes we see pheasant
basking in the ditch, see fresh

mountains of dirt upstream instead,
our property up in the hills beyond.
I could hear the trackhoe digging last fall

when the wind was from the south,
pictured the blade of a dozer scraping
away the scene. The ice is green as bile

on this warm day. Depression glass
with cracks. The dugout, rumoured to be
the largest in these parts, is full of water.

The air was hazy, full of blowing snow.
The wind picked up my new garbage
mitts & threw

them on the ground. I'd boasted
about my shitty skates—
that had lasted me

since I was 19, skating
backwards like I was learning to walk
on ice—so they broke

at the edge of the duck pond.
I was surrounded by women, falling
on surfaces with no give.

I've developed a fear of falling
on ice—stories of poem-killing concussions
& legs broken in four places

circulating like corona. But sailing
along on water that is 70% waterfowl poop
& duckweed is as close

as I'll get to flying.

A vole shoots down a tree well
as I round the house, the same tree
where the shrike sits & waits I guess

for you, little vole, your future a hook
with no relation to me & my shovel
full of snow, though

perhaps thinking vole is enough
to ensure you & your flight
response will live on. The shovel—heavy

as I carry a lack of sleep around,
up half the night googling the volcanic
explosivity index & volcanic winter

while waiting to hear news
about the people of Tonga—
fills & empties, the surface

of the drift like cement, as they say
around here, breaking apart in chunks
that barely fit in my shovel.

I'm congested, conflating
extreme weather warnings
with record test positivity rates.

"Exposed skin will freeze
in 30 seconds." with "For every 1 case reported
there are 8–10 missed." We squint

at the freezerburnt sky

at the public health dashboard
& pull our daughter

from school. Classmates organize
a walkout for the first day back
after a post-Xmas week

of remote learning. Children-
of-the-Internet, they post protest chants
to IG: *We're your kids*

not your guinea pigs.
Lab classes, not lab rats.
I diffuse my airborne

anxiety with my Monday regular.
We'd just crossed the bridge
over the Assiniboine

when my friend looked back
& saw his daughter, on her way home
from school. She'd been 20 feet

behind us for 10 minutes, jacket
unzipped. She tells him
she wouldn't have said anything

if he hadn't seen her, in the easily-spooked
way of teenagers. He runs over
to hug her. The forecast says

there's a storm coming.

What is that? Elk? Fox? Weird bird?
H & I look at each other, our ears
& years of experience failing us.

Camera in hand, boots on, I walk out
alone, H keeping watch, & head toward
a place gone quiet, through unbroken

snow, sinking to shin, knee, not quite hip
as I push through the trees,
two chickadees cheering my advance.

Fresh tracks on the path at the Y.
Chokecherry twigs catch in my hair
The tracks have a sinking urgency,

veering from one harey situation
to the next, marking piles of deadfall
on either side. Is the fox assessing my skills?

It's midnight, mid-January.
Outside, the wolf moon—
the freeze up / frost-exploding /severe moon—

rises unseen.
It's mid-winter, the season

of blood oranges & low light, for rosettes

of blue-green lichen & orange
bridge railings / rosehips,
the landscape a bleached tea-towel.

It's midnight on a Monday
& I wonder what happened
to my mother's raccoon-fur coat.

I would wear it now,
being equally rumpy /combative
in middle-age. Outside, a blizzard

has begun. It will dump
10–15 centimetres before it is done.
In the morning, my car

will be a suggestion. My front steps
will be a toboggan run.
Mid-January, I'm happy for every flake.

We need all the moisture
we can get, Manitoba's water table
set with millions of place settings.

The path to the house,
again a mountain range, peaks
the cat summits orange as the sun.

Seeing me at the window,
down the cat comes with claws
dug into the face of the drift,

fur puffed against the sifting snow,
tail twitching, indignant yet pleased
I'm in waiting. Watching how it's done.

Morning, reading flood forecasts
when my attic-dwelling daughter shouts
down the stairs: "MUM COME KILL

THE SPIDER
ON THE WALL ABOVE MY BED."
She appears on the kitchen threshold

without socks, force-feeds me
footage of a wolf spider & its shadow,
running away from her

& then a viral tik-tok
of a new tofu recipe. I tell her
I am philosophically-opposed to killing

spiders, trot out the old saw:
"You are never more
than ten feet from a spider."

I don't tell her a friend posted pics

of a coyote across the street
from her kids' school. It's no secret

we had very little rain,
Lake Manitoba reporting
record lows. Summers with no

mosquitoes but also no mushrooms
until the fall rains, stunted grain
mired in mud. Mid-January

& elsewhere-friends have
already posted, "Oh! It's almost spring!"
alongside sepia-toned photos,

all their snow melted. My response?
"WE HAD 15 CM LAST NIGHT!"
My daughter makes me safe-walk her

back to her bedroom,
demanding to know where
the spider is. I glance at her piles

of dirty laundry
meaningfully,

hopefully.

Everything is on paws since

witnessing the pursuit yesterday,
the coyotes flying, flushing two

more from the bush who looked over
their shoulders as they split up
& ran this way, likely to redirect

the danger onto the slow & fleshy
form ever glued to the window
should it ever step out.

Ravens filed in later, one by one,
circling the place & winding down
to take in an end I couldn't see

from where I tend to stand.
A few ravens continue today.
One passes by when I open the door,

make the journey across a deck
windswept
hammerheads waiting for a hip.

The mail truck isn't coming today,
the postmaster posts from a village
I can see if I squint. Too icy.

Gobbling from snowy street
to icy alley—my goal a wild turkey

grid search with all

the trimmings:
big flakes of snow
drifting down like down

after a pillow fight, trees
with flocks of sparrows
for leaves, wild turkeys roosting

everywhere. Instead, I hobbled
along, unable to locate
road or curb or sidewalk. Everything made

of snow. Then my snowpants
started to slide down like down
low & the woman walking

snow-silent behind me laughed
when I pulled up my coat
to better hike up

my puffy pants.
"Whoa!" she said,
stepping in my footsteps.

Dark when I wake up. Cold
as a thawed turkey, but likely not dead
for I hear H in the other room

giving our land location & asking
when the first call came in.
I'm more sure I'm alive

when my phone dings, a text from mom
asking if the power is out here too.
I get up, reach into the closet

for the Coleman lantern
then quickly dress, my shadow
spiriting the ceiling.

Two hoodies later I'm in the front room
& in the glow of the kerosene heater
checking temperatures,

Bios technology telling me
the pump house is plus 6 & the chicken house
where the barn cats are cuddled up is currently

warmer than here. It's -15 outside
not counting the wind. H sits plastic
jugs of milk & leftover roast beef in Pyrex

outside on the iron bench.
If need be, in an hour he'll head outside
to fire up the generator

& head across the road to fire up
a kerosene heater in the pump house

to keep the water lines from freezing.

I need to learn
how to fuel things up. In the east
an orange line thickens on the horizon.

Supply chain issues, yes, grocery shelves
half empty, but also: dump trucks
all over the city, hauling

snow to the depot. Everything's a snow-route
parking ticket in midwinter.
"Know your zone,"

the city begs homeowners,
then gets out the 4 am tow-trucks,
the front-end loaders,

groaning machines.
Everything's a car-killing berm.

Two sharp-tailed grouse on the fire guard
fight the wind, gusting to 70,
the temperature above zero again,

flurries about to begin. I read a letter
posted in the farmer's group,
address blacked out,

saying there wasn't enough rain last year
to facilitate breakdown
of certain herbicide residues

& the risk to sensitive
rotational crops. Following
in bold is a list of sprays & what

the farmer should NOT plant in 2022
depending on the soil zone.
According to the legend

our zone is brown meaning no
canola, durum wheat, or canary seed
if I understand right. I don't

understand why the grouse
leave themselves so exposed. Snow
is starting to fall. Comments follow.

Today, the temp is supposed to leap
from -14 to 0. I text my daughter
that she's walking home from school.

Her response? "I guess
I'll just SUFFER then!!"
I send GIFs instead of guff. An hour later,

I am summoned, after her third

135

fall-to-her-knees on the ice.
When I pull up,

she is clothed
in a layer of blowing snow, hatless,
her jacket flapping open.

Her big Dr. Marten boots
that make her taller than me
betrayed her on the ice,

but that's a practically a prairies-kid
rite of passage, like frostbitten
earlobes or winter Slurpees, garbage mitts

covered in ink. My parents
would have pointedly not
answered the phone.

Coyotes call from the hills west
at the ever-shrinking sunset.
A great-horned owl hoots

across the hollow like it knows
I have less friends than an hour ago.
To the south three wind towers blink, red

eyes of baby mice. I'm not used to them yet,
would not want to be any closer...on & on

goes my inner NIMBY. Across the river

the three blink,
as if looking at each other in disbelief.
It's unanimous. I have less friends

but it's nice outside, nicer than inside
where the smell of fish still lingers.
It's hard to think good things

about that purple scribble on the orange
skyline. Polarized? It looks as if
someone is desperate to roll out some ink.

Forget it, the pen is dry. It's quiet now
& growing dark fast.
The owl could hoot again any time.

A wasp's nest missing its dingy
wrapping sways like a piñata
in the bare branches

most of the way to Omand's Creek.
I always want to knock down
their papier-mache

constructions,
pulp scraped from picnic tables
& balconies. I inhabit

the millions of years
between carnivorous wasps
& vegetarian bees, diverging

in the mid-Cretaceous. I am comforted
that wasps probably buzzed
the mouths, the inner arms

& fingers (talons? claws?) of feeding
dinosaurs too. Further along,
a round metal ball

topped with a spike
on the roof of a house. "I bet
it's a lightning rod," M says. I want it

to be a homemade onion dome.
The ones on Ukrainian
orthodox churches in the North End

make me ache. I always miss
their all-you-can-eat
perogy (pierogi? pirohy?)

dinners, but I am stuck—
like a butcher bird stowing
a songbird on a bit of barbed wire—

on the idea of a bunch
of old women, shaping dough

in a church kitchen.

I'm struck by work bees, voices
raised in song, the moment
at a reading where

you can hear people listening.
We walk on.

Sunrise, a soft orange
twenty deer pull apart
as they walk this way

down the road, pausing
now & then between
ditches full of snow,

between barbed wire fences,
the neighbour's on the right,
ours on the left which I'll cut

out of the pic I post
for the sake of composition.
To keep the image quiet

I'll forgo any language
leaps in the caption,
avoid any near-rhymes

with insurrection or sedition,
won't mention the grader
coming over the hill, plowing

snow, the twenty double-takes,
the leaps
& bounds that follow

through the ditch & over the fence.
The deer slow. The grader passes.
I wave at the driver.

Fuck yes hi
is what my voice-to-text software
hears when a leashed dog bursts

out of a backdoor, barking,
& I surprise-*screeeeeeeeeeeam*, one hand
on my phone, the other

on my heart. I stumble
down the sleet-soaked street,
my glasses looking

like I've been crying,
like someone got close & carefully
spat in each eye. "Turkey's behind

our place, if you're interested,"

is what my poet-friend down the street
texted this morning,

between slicing green apples
for my daughter's lunch
& my first meeting of the day.

I'm stalking the alleys mid-afternoon,
aware that I've been caught
on security cameras. I peer in garages

& backyards, but snow-buried
second cars, squirrels
& sparrows mobbing

feeders, taking refuge on fencelines
& in leafless lilacs, are all I find.
Today, someone told me a cougar had been

spotted in Wolseley. I wanted
to make a joke about my neeeeeeeeeeeds

but I knew they meant coyotes.

The weather is changing.
Sixty deer gather on the hill line.
Rough count. Last night I looked up

Ram Ranch, Frozen, white hats,

astroturfing, rent-a-mobs, & now
The Emergencies Act. Happy

Valentine's Day! It feels
like I'm at the back of the class
preparing for show & tell

& have forgotten what to say.
It's noon. The herd, mostly mule deer
with white-tailed on the side,

begin to move again, hopefully away
from our young apple trees
& plumping lilacs. The silent majority

disappear one by one over the hill
to where the spray plane crashed
years back with its payload of Lorsban.

After a snowfall
I don't clear off the roof
of my car, only enough to get me on

the road: the windshield, rear-view
window & front side windows.
I like watching snow blow

off my car in traffic, while
accelerating or caught in a cross-wind.

My neighbours mow

my boulevard. I forget hostess gifts.
I gnaw in my friends'
spotless cars. I bicker with M

about whose turn
it is to shovel the front steps.
We are shamed

into action by entrepreneurial
teens, who shovel for cash.
My coup-de-gras?

The letter carrier will skip us
if our steps aren't shovelled
& M orders a LOT of things online.

We are running out
of places to put snow.

The petunia seeds are pelleted,
yellow & easy to press
into the soil as instructed,

in this case the premium organic
seed starter mix I use to fill
each of the 36 cells per tray

which I spray
then cover with vented domes
& place on heat mats in bright light

to aid germination. If someone happened
to go by on the road they'd see me
alone at a south-facing window

of a snow-bound house
in hills known for rock
more valuable than I knew.

I have set up a puzzle table
in my office at a right angle to my desk.
We have 156.6 cm of snow,

most of it on my garage
roof. I am not normally
a roof-raker but this is a jalopy garage

dating back to 1912. We use it to store
boxes of junk we were too tired
to unpack

when we moved here in 2009.
I feel like weeping
when I see Ontario's primroses,

BC's snowdrops. We took

five bags of clothes
& two bins of books

to Value Village & felt lighter.
But my puzzle table
was a bad decision. I have to crawl

under it to leave the room.
(It doesn't show on Zoom.)

I want to note the moose
running this way
from the south

sticking to the hilltops
where there's less snow.
I wonder if it was spooked

too by the fighter jet that went
over a short while ago,
probably a training flight

from the base in Moose Jaw.
It sounded low, chewed its way
through my skull. Please door,

don't stick. I want a clearer pic.
I turn the knob, the latch clicks,
hinges squeak. The moose stops

in the extreme cold & looks
straight at me, incredulous, ears
overturned in my rapid

paddle across the deck,
the rubber soles of my slippers
sticking to the ice

as the moose raises its head,
noses the cold like it can
smell the sheet pan chicken

warming in the microwave.

I wake up at 4:30 am, convinced
that it's time to herd
twenty-four

creative writing students
into Assiniboine Forest. *Two plus hours*
early, stupid brain! I'd asked

for snowpants & boots
but there is still someone wearing
sneakers & ankle socks

in snow stacked to mid-calf:
"I thought I WAS dressed warmly."
I deal out handwarmers like

winning hands and then ask:
What does it feel like
to be enclosed by clones?

What does it feel like
to be surrounded?
Everything grey/white,

I ask them to find colour
in the winter forest, standing next to
an incandescent clump

of red dogwood,
my eyes darting to a trembling
aspen with a thin coat

of yellow lichen. "For my next trick,
I'll need a volunteer!" I intone.
We topple backwards

into snowbanks once,
then again. Synchonized snow angel-ing!
My pockets fill with powder,

I struggle out of the drifts, but refuse
a hand up. My logic?
If you regularly throw yourself

into snowbanks,
you have to be able

to winch yourself out.

A deer bounds across the board-
hard drift, breaks through & sinks
to its belly. The herd looks on,

weary, I expect, down as they are
to their last antler, one left
antler to be exact, on the head

of a surly-looking buck.
When the antler falls it's called
a shed, a shed in the path

of a two-hundred-dollar tire
when we head to town
in the middle of the freeze part

of the freeze-thaw cycle.
The buck puts its ears back
when the lead deer stamps its feet.

The one up to its belly
stots three times
& it's out.

A friend posts
that she walked her big dog

on the Assiniboine River & fell

through the ice, simultaneously
soaked & frostbitten, fingers scizing.
Weeks of -30, snow filling

backyards & blocking back doors,
but the province, wary
of spring

flooding, opened
the Shellmouth Reservoir, under-
mining the ice from below.

So: knee-high slush
& open water under all
that snow. We are close

to breaking
the snowfall record, after years
of not getting anywhere

close. The local river trail group wails
that all its equipment
is still on the ice: 6 sawhorses,

12 shovels, 6 benches, solar-powered
lighting & miscellaneous
signage. It sounds

like an insurance claim. A final
report. My failure? I respond
to my friend's plea

that someone do *something*
before someone dies,
with a link to this year's

Shellmouth Reservoir
press release, my sympathy
a soaked boot, a questionable

claim to public space.

A gravel truck goes by.
Then another
hauling

grey loads of crushed rock
from somewhere in the hills
to somewhere near the river I guess

going by the length of time
between passings. One of the trucks
crawls by quietly, kicking up little snow,

the other one is all brum bum bum
bum bum *as it shifts down*
right in front of our place, farting diesel,

the driver hating our quiet existence
or loving the powerful engine
or both. I take pics

with the big camera, zoom
in on the plates & loads,
telling myself I was young once too.

It's a quiet day otherwise.
A light breeze. The sun is shaking
sparkles off the trees.

February sun through a south-facing
window spreads itself,
yellow tablecloth, over the desk

in this borrowed office. Radiant heat
has me in shirtsleeves. I need a plant,
something living in here

besides me, something forgiving.
Out my breadbox window, the spread
of an old tree, bare

& broken branches up
high. Twenty feet away, a sapling
in a bad spot, its central leader broken,

mired in snow like a horse in a blizzard.

The administrator confides
that they keep on planting new trees

in the same place, a map somewhere
reading X-marks-the-spot.
Except X is code

for bad drainage & drought. They come by
every few years to plant a new tree.
I want to organize

a tree-watering committee, dragging
hose out between buildings. I want
to whittle a spear.

February is Feb bee wary
from now on! The buzzer
hits the window like a game

show contestant. "Is that a leaf
cutter bee?" I ask H as he traps it
in a plastic container

& puts it in the fridge to photograph
later when the bee has cooled down.
It looks like the ones who carved

circles out of dogwood leaves
near the house last summer, folded

them like tortilla breakfast wraps

& flew off to build their nests,
some, I see now, in pots of red geraniums
I brought in to overwinter. Blooming

garish condos. Time shares
secrets, possible stings. Check the cushions
before I sit down, shake out the bedding,

check the sleeves of my parka.
A dozen bees now.
The other day I watched one haul

its striped abdomen across the maple
floor, collecting dust as it went.
The dust eventually slowed it down.

-30 C all week but I need
to go gawk at the snow depot hills
before the melt

sets in. The sun in the frozen
sky has changed, yellow & low & warm.
I need buy plus-sized

chest-waders in some inoffensive
camo print before the rush.
I should go look at the rings

in the clawtooth bathtub
of the Shellmouth Reservoir, released
water flowing through

the Assiniboine & up the Red,
as spring meltwater fires up
the floodplain.

Come March, I will monitor
the banks of the Red for shards
of milkglass

& formerly-frosty beer bottles
to prise from the ground,
hundred-year-old threats

about copyright & returning bottles
clear in the mud. They only ever
rented out the contents.

I have embraced my second-hand
existence, but floating
plastics undercut

my argument. I promise
Mike I'll be careful
around the floodwaters.

A pack of five coyotes

154

advance on the slough,
push up the hill & head north.

Something is going to die.
Now sharp-tailed grouse
move in. We count fifty-five,

the biggest flock we've seen.
They run around like ants
on a pile of sugar.

There's a porcupine
in the cottonwood right now
chewing the bark off a branch

hanging over the road. Careful, now.
If it breaks, the porcupine could take out
a windshield.

On the sidewalk, where they've scraped
down to the asphalt, piling
the debris on the boulevard—

compressed layers of snow
& sand that have most of the winter
in each chunk. Seasonable fossils?

Ephemeral agates? I am tempted
to take away some of the snowcrete

& build a bunker.

It was a cold winter: 14 blizzards,
100 missiles arcing between Russia
& Ukraine, 272 convoy truckers arrested

in Ottawa. I hear there's still room
for snowmelt infiltration.
I'm hoping for a gentle thaw.

One coyote lies down
& pants while another marks
the snow & another sniffs the air

with its tongue sticking out
like a thermometer, red tip a tail-
length away from all it desires.

We saw a pack in Bone Coulee too
on our way home from town, one coyote
lying down as if hot & spent.

Coyote pups in 63 days I predict
after I google gestation
instead of nuclear winter

like I did last night before taking
my blood pressure. I post
one of the few tongueless pics,

less lust & more happiness,
my contribution to the procreative
prairie propaganda machine.

Yippee! It's after dinner & dark
when a poet-friend texts me.
The Lenore turkey is roosting behind

her place! I might see her
tomorrow if I'm up early enough.
"It's been a while since she slept over,"

she writes, as if the bird
was her daughter's bestie. I wake
to her update: *bzzt.* "Turkey is up!"

bzzt. "Oh, just stretching."
It's almost eight am when I lurch down
the alley. The hen is a big

football in the bare branches
of the neighbour's Manitoba maple,
tarnished keys

rattling in the breeze.
Her head tucked under her wing.
Body brown with streaks of blue & pink.

Wings are buff & brown

157

like the tail of a raptor. I loiter
under sprays

of tiny red crabapples,
as people take the garbage out, drive
to work. My friend comes out

& tells me of the gendered poops
of turkeys—males make Js, females Ses—
then goes back in.

The bird grooms herself
before settling down for another snooze.
Icicles hanging from every roofline.

Sparrows chirp.
Before, I only wanted to catch
a glimpse. Now I am

apparently waiting for her
to descend from the tree,
to perform her turkey-ness.

My fingers are cold.

I head home.

The porcupine, back
in the cottonwood & big

as my circle,

looks as though it rolled
through rusty needles in a post-
apocalyptic acupuncture clinic.

Its teeth are red
as the horizon at sundown
when a system moves in.

A quick search tells me what I see
is actually reddish-orange, normal,
due to iron oxide in the enamel.

How did I get to be this age
without knowing better
the teeth of friends & neighbours?

ACKNOWLEDGMENTS

This book was written during the pandemic, when everything changed and everything stayed the same. I was used to working from home, but suddenly, I was home ALL the time and so was my teenage daughter, with my photojournalist partner coming and going, his shoulders around his ears from not having his work-life change.

I coped by going outside, because that was the only activity available to me, the only safe space. I walked every Monday with John Toews and every Sunday with Matt Joudrey, both of whom I've worked with to publish and launch books but who are just as important to me as friends. Many of the poems in this collection came out of the adventures we had on those walks.

During this period, I had the great good luck to receive three arts grants—from the Winnipeg and Manitoba Arts Councils and the Canada Council for the Arts.

My evergreen thanks to my partner Mike and daughter Anna for joining me in this life as a full-time poetry cult recruiter.

In spring 2021, I did a residency at the Buller Greenhouse at the University of Manitoba, thanks to MAC funding and the goodwill of Jo-Anne Joyce and Carla Dale. The Buller Greenhouse is one of my favourite places and I miss being able to dip into its humid airspace, being able to put down my gak and go see what was blooming.

I returned to UManitoba in winter 2022 when we were writing the last poems in *Siteseeing*, working as Writer-in-Residence at the Centre for Creative Writing and Oral Culture. I deeply appreciated the help/insight from CCWOC director/writer Jocelyn Thorpe and Mary Elliott. I am also grateful to St. John's College for providing an office, yet again, so I had a different window to look out of.

I would like to thank the members of the Electronic Garret, who saw many of these poems in draft during NaPoWriMo but particularly Maureen Hynes, Micheline Maylor, Tanis MacDonald, and Kerry Ryan.

I am exceedingly grateful to Bren Simmers, who edited this book. She has been the greatest of colleagues since we met at Sage Hill in 2003 and I'm so excited to see what she does next!

Sue Sorensen, Erna Buffie, and Lauren Carter have saved

me so many times, with good advice, commiseration, and bad ideas. Here's to many more years of the same! Thanks to Sally Ito for the mudlarking show-and-tell, Ken Stewart and James Duncan for the owl know-how, and Kerry Ryan for sharing her turkey hen.

Beyond that, I would like to thank Brenda Schmidt for everything. I am honoured to have had the chance to write with her: she is better and smarter than me but she is still my friend and colleague.

No, Ariel is better and smarter than me! She has the energy of a southerly wind during spring migration. Thank you to Ariel for so generously carrying me along over the years.
April is nearing its end as I write this. Today a Say's phoebe arrived on said wind, northerly now, and perched on a burnt hydrant across the road, pumping its tail as it hunted for bugs. With camera in hand, I hid behind the chicken house (now cat house – thank you Uber and Roamer for your friendship) and watched its rhythm until I had it down, hoping I'd finally get some decent pics of this prairie bird. When it dove for a fly, I advanced three steps. It let me do this three times. I thank the phoebe for humoring me.

Thank you to At Bay Press for their vision and being wonderful to work with. Thank you to Bren Simmers for her brilliant edit.

Thank you to the amazing Electronic Garret.

As always, thank you to my family.

No one has humored me for as long as my partner Harvey has. Thank you. More than three decades later, we're still one-upping each other in the hermit department, thankful for each adventure together, and thankful for this place and everything that lives here in whatever way it does. Even the grasshoppers.

Poems from this manuscript appeared in *Understorey's* Rural & Remote Living special issue and as part of the League of Canadian Poets' *Poetry Pause and PRISM International's* Grouse Grind Lit Prize. Our thanks to the editors of these publications!

Photo: Mike Deal

ARIEL GORDON (she/her) is a Winnipeg/Treaty 1 territory-based a writer, editor, and enthusiast. She is the ringleader of Writes of Spring, a National Poetry Month project with the Winnipeg International Writers Festival that appears in the *Winnipeg Free Press*. Her first two collections of poetry won the Lansdowne Prize for Poetry. Her most recent books are the essay collection *Treed: Walking in Canada's Urban Forests* (Wolsak & Wynn, 2019) and the first book in the public poetry project *TreeTalk* (At Bay Press, 2020), which was nominated for three Manitoba Book Awards. In 2022, her work appeared in *Canadian Notes and Queries, Canthius, periodicities*, and *The Quarantine Review.*

Photo: Harvey Schmidt

BRENDA SCHMIDT was the seventh Saskatchewan Poet Laureate. Author of five books of poetry and a book of essays, her work has been nominated for Saskatchewan Book Awards, received the Alfred G. Bailey Prize for Poetry, and is included in *The Best of the Best Canadian Poetry in English: Tenth Anniversary Edition*. Over the years she has served on the board of directors of the Saskatchewan Writers' Guild and Sage Hill Writing, and more recently as poetry editor for *Grain*. She gardens on a dry hillside in central west Saskatchewan in Treaty 6 territory, and has several rain barrels.

OUR AT BAY PRESS
ARTISTIC COMMUNITY:

Publisher - **Matt Joudrey**
Managing Editor - **Alana Brooker**
Substantive Editor - **Bren Simmers**
Copy/Proof Editor - **Priyanka Ketkar**
Graphic Designer - **Matt Stevens**
Cover Artist - **Matt Joudrey**

Thanks for purchasing this book and for supporting authors and artists. As a token of gratitude, please scan the QR code for exclusive content from this title.